THE JOY THAT IS IN ME

THE LIFE AND THOUGHT OF ELISABETH LESEUR

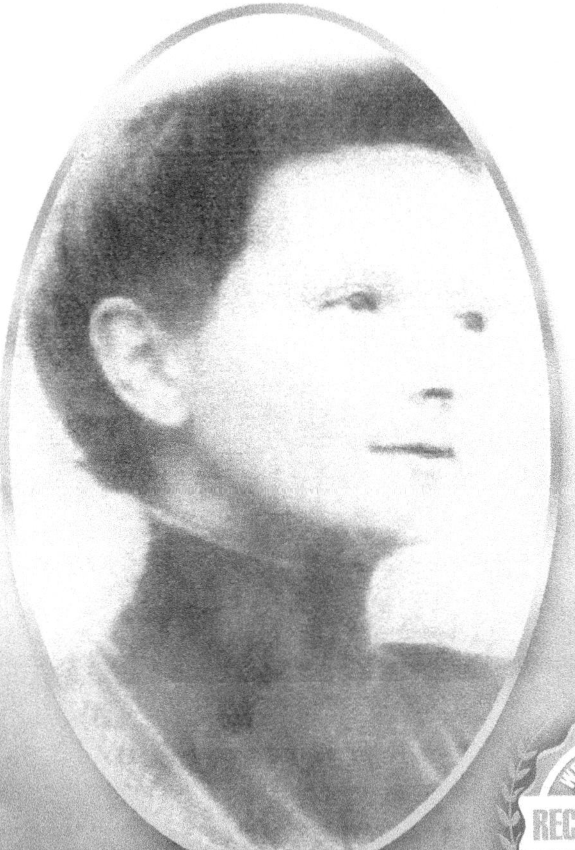

JENNIFER MOORCROFT

WORKBOOK PRESS LLC
187 E Warm Springs Rd,
Suite B285, Las Vegas, NV 89119, USA

Website: https://workbookpress.com/
Hotline: 1-888-818-4856
Email: admin@workbookpress.com

Ordering Information:
Quantity sales. Special discounts are available on quantity purchases by corporations, associations, and others.
For details, contact the publisher at the address above.

Library of Congress Control Number:
ISBN-13:   978-1-955459-88-4 (Paperback Version)
                978-1-955459-89-1 (Digital Version)

REV. DATE: 14/06/2021

THE JOY THAT IS IN ME

The life and thought of the Servant of God, Elisabeth Leseur

Jennifer Moorcroft

CONTENTS

INTRODUCTION

'By their fruits you shall know them,' our Saviour has said – by the fruits of devotion, charity, and radiant faith, and also by those flowers that first strike the eye and precede the fruit; those flowers are called sweetness, charm, nobility and exterior distinction of manners and ways, serenity, equanimity, friendliness, smiles and simplicity.

A deep and sanctified soul – perfect mistress, by divine grace, of the body and its obstacles – such a soul, without ever pouring itself out, shines forth and sheds upon everything the delicate perfume of these flowers of which I speak. Such a one attracts hearts and by its gentle influence prepares them for the coming of the Master, which she obtains for them eventually by her prayers.[1]

Elisabeth Leseur wrote these words in her 'Secret Diary', found only after her death in 1914, a diary which with other writings has influenced, guided and enriched souls ever since. She was describing the life she was striving to live, but also at the same time describing so well her own self.

For all her married life, her husband, Félix, who had become atheist when studying medicine in Paris, ridiculed and derided the faith that was so precious to her. She lived in an atmosphere that was hostile to her Catholic Faith, so she was very rarely able to speak openly of it. Therefore, she would allow her life to speak, a life that was dogged by ill health, which she united with her ever deepening prayer life, for the conversion of her husband, and for souls. Her love of God flowed out, too, in charity work among the poorest in the Paris slums.

The Cause for her beatification and canonisation has once again been opened by the Dominican Order, and it is hoped that many will be inspired by the beauty of her life and the inspiration of her writings.

PART 1

CHAPTER 1

EARLY LIFE

Elisabeth Leseur was born into wealth and privilege among the Paris aristocracy. Her father, Antoine Arrighi, from a wealthy Corsican family, came to Paris to complete his law studies and obtained a doctorate in law; he then entered the Paris bar. He was esteemed for his brilliant intellect but even more for his integrity, his goodness and charm, something that was also true of her mother, Gatienne Marie-Laure Picard, a cultivated woman, intelligent and passionate, a worthy match for her older husband,. Their home on the rue Baillif was a magnet for Parisian society, from, of course, the law, but also from the arts, politics, poetry, music, travel, the theatre and the universities. It was into this vibrant milieu that Elisabeth was born, 16 October 1866, and was baptised in the parish church of Saint-Roch 27 November. Their parents went on to have four more children. Amélie, the only boy, Pierre, Juliette and Marie, the youngest.

All the children were initially taught at home by the de Mas sisters, Louise and Amélie, whose well-to-do family had fallen on hard times. They were excellent teachers, Louise concentrating on music and the piano, which Elisabeth loved, and Amélie teaching such subjects as foreign languages, painting, history, geography and mathematics. She had, too, the stimulating atmosphere of their home and the wide variety of friends who met there.

When she was 11 years old and preparing to make her First Holy Communion Elisabeth began to keep a diary; it gives a picture of a lively, strong-willed and intelligent girl who was only too aware of her faults, her 'spirit of contradiction', her unwillingness to admit when she was in the wrong and her tendency to being a tease; her brother Pierre was mostly the butt of her teasing and also of their quarrels. 'I was naughty yesterday, a Sunday!' she noted in her diary. 'I quarrelled with Pierre. Oh, it's horrible being eleven years old'. Although, because she afterwards apologised to him, she knew the good God would forgive her. When the catechism classes began the parish priest, M Séguin, told them that they would be making their first Confession. Elisabeth was happy, for, as she said, 'I have great need of it!'; she found it a very moving experience and not in the least intimidating.

Their father was by now a nominal Catholic, attending Mass with the family only on special occasions, and with no religious commitment. It was their mother who guided the children in their first steps in the faith, teaching them their prayers, how to make the sign of the cross and going with them to Mass. She was a fervent Catholic and took a great interest in preparing Elisabeth for her First Communion, sometimes going with her to the catechism classes and overseeing her homework afterwards.

In her diary Elisabeth mentioned more and more her longing to receive Holy Communion; the great day 18 May, was preceded by a three-day retreat. Elisabeth wrote a detailed account of it, revelling in the time she was able to spend in church:

> How good this retreat is, above all because we can be in church, we sing, we pray, we meditate, we are wholly focused on the good God; but, at home, I have made myself a little altar where I pray and read. I enjoy this solitude, alone with the good God.[2]

This passage shows how far her spiritual life had already developed. She was able, even as a twelve-year-old, to remain at peace in the presence of God; she makes the distinction between vocal prayer and the meditation to which it should lead. She had also made a private space, in a lively household, where she could be alone with God. At the end of the day, when she received her Lord in Holy Communion for the first time she wrote:

> It is over! The beautiful day of my First Communion has passed. … How can I express the bliss I tasted at that moment! I possessed Our Lord, he was in me, I was no longer alone, I was with Our Lord…. Yes, the day of First Communion is truly the most beautiful day in life.[3]

The following day she received Confirmation, 'and now all these joys are over. But I really hope I can renew them often'.

Life returned to normal; there were lessons, trips out to the theatre and visits to make. The de Mas sisters opened classes in the rue du Mail at this time, so the Arrighi girls then went there for lessons instead of at home. Elisabeth worked hard at subjects that interested her, such as history and geography; her liveliness, intelligence and amazing memory, something she inherited from her mother, made up for her lack of application in the rest such as French grammar. Their parents arranged for trips out for the children to the nearby Bois de Boulogne, to Saint-Cloud, to the theatre to see plays. Besides their regular holidays at their holiday home in Auteuil, they went to various places in France and Switzerland; Elisabeth had a life-long love of travel.

As she grew older she took her part in the intellectual stimulation that surrounded her at home. However, she wasn't so keen on learning how to run a household of her own once she married. She made resolutions and forgot them, much to her mother's annoyance, who took her aside one day and spoke sternly to her about her behaviour, the way she wasn't taking her studies seriously enough and not helping enough in the home. Elisabeth herself was only too aware of her faults, as she noted in her diary.:

> My God, how bad I am! I wasn't kind yesterday evening. Me, I never think about what I'm doing, I'm preoccupied with knowing what's best for me, if it will be useful. I never try to talk, to be amiable and, if Mother makes observations, I show impatience and bad temper. Oh! It's so bad to be like that! I really would like to correct myself, but it is so difficult. I am making a resolution to do what I can to change and ask the good God to help me. I will pay attention to everything that's going on around me, I will talk, I will be pleasant. My God, help me, I pray; Saint Mary, pray for me.[4]

To help Elisabeth, they agreed on a plan:

> She told me that it was about time that I worked seriously, that every day I should take just one thing but do it very regularly and, when I forget to do it, I should write it in my diary since, once I get into the habit of doing one thing I can

then take on something else to do.

> I'm making the resolution: I'm going to ask Mother to tell me what thing I should do. I will try to do it every day and, if I fail, I will write it in my diary and try to do better another time.[5]

She was as good as her word and noted down every time she failed during that month of September. She finally stopped writing in her diary in March 1881. Her efforts were paying off, and she was beginning to blossom into the lovely young woman they both wanted. However, the family was scarred by two events that would have lasting consequences. Staying in Saint-Aubin in 1887 Elisabeth became seriously ill with typhoid fever. Earlier on she had contracted hepatitis, which from then on would flare up from time to time; both illnesses would have repercussions throughout her life. Then her youngest sister, the charming and gentle Marie who was only twelve years old and who had made her First Communion only two months earlier, also contracted typhoid, and died on 5 July. As Elisabeth was to write later:

> She closed her beautiful eyes, full of tenderness, on the vision of things that pass, and opened her soul completely to the vision and the possession of that which lasts eternally.[6]

Though their strong Christian faith helped the close-knit family through the enormous void of Marie's death, it still left a raw and agonising pain in their hearts. As Elisabeth wrote a month later to a friend:

> You know how much affection I have for you and so it takes all my courage to write to you today. In thinking of you, I can't help remembering that last time we spent together, for us a complete happiness that we had enjoyed until then. It is only a month since then, we were united, happy, in good health, and today we are in Mussey, aunt is in Paris, and our dear little Marie is in heaven … this is hard, very hard for us who were so united; I am not ungrateful to God, for we have immense consolations.

> Nothing was more peaceful, more gentle than the departure of that little soul; she slipped away without suffering into the

arms of the good God. At the last moment she opened her eyes with a smile that remained after her death.[7]

She described how beautiful her little sister looked, dressed in the veil she had worn for her First – and last – Holy Communion. They were not allowed to say goodbye to her before her death for fear of being infected with the dread disease, which was an added sorrow. They left Paris shortly after the funeral to stay with a friend, Mme Duboys, to escape 'the noise that is so odious to us' as Elisabeth put it, and to recover a little from their loss. Elisabeth never fully recovered from the death of her beloved sister, but it would become a vital element in her profound belief in the Communion of Saints that later on became so important to her.

CHAPTER 2

MARRIAGE

Through their contacts in legal circles, the Arrighis were close friends with the Gavignots, who were also close friends of the Leseur family. When therefore, the Leseur's younger son, Félix, wanted to study medicine at the Faculty of Medicine in Paris, M Leseur wrote to the Gavignots asking them to take him under their wing.

It was only a matter of time before Elisabeth and Félix would meet each other; this occurred one evening at a soirée at the Gavignot's. Mme Gavignot said that the chemistry between the two was so immediate, so electric, that the whole room felt it. Elisabeth had just turned 21 and Félix was five years older. He later recalled that his first impressions of Elisabeth was that she was physically very charming, very agreeable, very distinguished in her bearing and her ways. Talking to her, Félix found that she was also very cultured and that her mind was open to everything, with an intelligence that was remarkably quick and penetrating. She was especially interested in the arts, in literature and music. He was immediately drawn to her by her vivacity and her joyousness.

As for Elisabeth, her heart was totally taken by this dapper young doctor, always immaculately dressed, always bright, cheerful and enthusiastic. They soon found that they had a great deal in common, and Elisabeth's sister, Amelie, remarked that 'they are so boring, they talk about Wagner all the time!'

They were officially engaged 23 May 1889, to the delight of both their families. They were married in their parish church of Saint-Germain-de-Prés, 31 July 1889. One of Félix's former schoolmasters officiated, the Oratorian Fr Bordes, for whom Félix had a great respect, and who had had a great influence on him. According to French law, they then had a civil marriage at the Place Saint-Sulpice and left in the afternoon for Fontainbleau and their new life together.

Writing to her uncle Alexandre, of their trip down the Rhine, Elisabeth said, 'All this ravished me; all the time we were in such a delight and unimaginable silliness, and if there were two people on earth most happy, it was us'.[8] Soon after their return, though, Elisabeth developed an abdominal abscess, which could lead to peritonitis, usually fatal at that time. Then in December her father died suddenly. Elisabeth was too ill to attend his funeral and watched the cortège from her bedroom window. She was bedridden for several months, and because of her internal problems the young couple were given the devastating news that Elisabeth would never be able to have children. This was an abiding sorrow, especially for Elisabeth, and one that she would come to terms with in her own special way.

She also had time to reflect on her relationship with Félix, who had thrown up some disturbing revelations about himself only a short while before their wedding. Despite his esteem for Fr Bordes and having a nuptial Mass, Félix had confided in her that he no longer believed in the Catholic faith. During his medical studies his faith had been undermined and then destroyed by the materialistic milieu of the university and the prevailing anti-clerical and anti-Catholic atmosphere by which he was surrounded. He had quickly lapsed first into paganism and then into atheism.

Although this had distressed Elisabeth greatly, she had consented to their marriage on the understanding that he would allow her to practise her faith. He was soon going back on this promise. Félix had a deep interest in the French colonies, and became an expert on the subject, writing for journals which were also anti-Catholic, becoming editor in two of them. He was mixing with politicians and journalists who had a real hatred of anything Catholic. This had a marked effect on him, hardening his atheistic beliefs. Until then he had tolerated Elisabeth's faith, but now he began to be increasingly intolerant of anything that contradicted his atheism; he was convinced there could be no neutrality between the two, that neutrality was either a myth or a deception. 'It is possible, if need be, sometimes but very rarely, to be tolerant and to give the illusion of it,' he wrote, 'but to be neutral – never!'[9]

Félix soon made Elisabeth herself the object of his proselytizing, stocking their library with atheistic writers, but he found that there was an easier way to detach his wife from her Christian roots. They both loved socialising, going to the theatre, art galleries and restaurants, enjoying the social round of their class. Their house was a magnet for the highest in Parisian society, from writers, musicians and artists, politicians and journalists; unbelief and anti-clericalism was almost a given among them. Elisabeth had almost no time to cultivate that inner silence in which she could pray and revive herself spiritually. It was with satisfaction, therefore, that from 1891, little by little, Félix noted that Elisabeth began losing the practice of prayer that had been so much a part of her from her childhood. As he wrote later: 'The war that I waged against Elisabeth's beliefs found very favourable ground in this chaos' [10]

Félix had studied medicine, not for its own sake, but because he hoped it would lead to a post in the colonies. In 1893 he was offered a post in Africa, but Elisabeth's family were so concerned about the effect that living abroad would have on her precarious health that he gave up his dream and accepted a post in the family's insurance firm, the Conservatoire, becoming its director the following year.

In 1893, the couple were invited to join a pilgrimage to Rome, a visit they extended by going to the major cities of Italy. Félix had hoped that Elisabeth might find her faith weakened by seeing the splendours of the Vatican, which repulsed him, but instead, he saw her faith increase by being in the city where so many martyrs had lost their lives. Her faith was reignited, and Félix's antagonism increased.

They might not be going to settle in Africa, but both Elisabeth and Félix loved travelling. With Elisabeth in better health, in 1896 they travelled to Tunisia and Algeria and throughout Europe. Elisabeth's health improved in warm climates and she always loved light and colour. As Elisabeth described in her diary:

> At Carthage, in a carriage, having a superb view of the Gulf of Tunis throughout the journey. The weather is wonderful, and under the hot sun we contemplate beds of poppies, yellow daisies and brooms, which carry out their joyful role in the countryside. There are many olive trees and cactus surround the houses, which with their grey colouring offsets the radiance of the other colours …climbing the hill that was Byrsa, we saw stretched before us a panorama that we enjoyed today. Before us, always blue, was the Gulf vast and tranquil; behind us, Tunis, a patch of blazing white, always glittering under the

radiance of a sun that illuminates everything here. And, from distance to distance, other points of white in the greenness; these are the Arab villages scattered around the Gulf. [11]

They returned from their travels with Elisabeth renewed in body and spirit:

> This good life together, so liberating, so removed from the stifling conventions of the big city, so free from prejudices, this continual connection with great and beautiful nature, this contact with new art and a civilisation different from one's own, all this makes the trip wholly good and healthy, as good for the body which it develops and strengths and for the mind which it renews, enlightens and transforms. [12]

Elisabeth was a proud Frenchwoman, a proud Parisienne, who loved her country; these travels opened her eyes to other civilizations, cultures, beliefs and religions. With her openhearted response to life she recognised that if she was proud of who she was, of her country, then others had an equal right to be proud of who they were, in their background, country, beliefs. This had a profound effect on the sensitive way she would approach others who believed differently from her.

The following year Félix had to travel extensively throughout Europe on business, so Elisabeth went with them, taking in major cities on the way. The highlight for both of them, though, was their stay in Bayreuth and the opportunity for them to attend some of the performances. For Wagner-lovers, it was a delight. They even managed to go twice to the Ring performance, and twice to Parsifal. 'All of the best in us had been stirred', Elisabeth wrote in her diary; even Félix had been stirred, by a work that had a religious theme:

> The performance of Parsifal gave us hours of profound enjoyment. But one can't analyse such impressions. It seems to me that this would spoil them. I would say, simply, that in this admirable work, the religious sentiment was expressed in a way I had never before seen it in any other work, however great, and that one breathes in a divine perfume of forgiveness, love and purity which calms and stirs at the same time. [13]

Even an atheist can be moved by sublime music, even religious music, but Elisabeth herself still had remnants of her faith within her. Back home, they settled back into their usual routine, the social round in which they immersed themselves, only for Elisabeth to slip back into indifference towards her faith; as the new year arrived, Félix noted with satisfaction that he considered by now that his wife had abandoned her faith.

Having some time on her hands a short while afterwards Elisabeth asked Félix for something to read and from his large library he selected two books that he felt sure would destroy the last remnants of faith that remained in her. He gave her a copy of 'The Origins of Christianity' which he felt would give her a revulsion of Christianity when she read its history, and the 'Life of Jesus', which would expose the shaky credentials of the Gospels. Both of them were by Renan; his 'Life of Jesus' was already causing great upset in Cathoic circles, with many losing their faith, so Félix was confident that the same would happen to his wife.

CHAPTER 3

CONVERSION

Elisabeth read the two books, studying them carefully, and the result was the opposite of what Félix had intended. With her exceptional and balanced intellect, her sure judgement and excellent good sense, Elisabeth was able to see through Renan's essential weaknesses, his shallowness and the poverty of his reasoning, his often contradictory arguments and unsupported assertions. She turned to the Gospels, at first to counter his arguments, but then to be overwhelmed by their beauty and truth:

> I read the Gospel, and by that sweet light I discover in myself a nook of egotism and vanity. Unique book, perpetually read and perpetually new, supremely beautiful, resplendent with truth, of exquisite grace and charm, from which one can draw unendingly and never exhaust it![14]

She discovered again the person of Jesus Christ, and she would never again abandon Him. However, she realised what effect her new-found faith would have on her husband and for some time didn't reveal to him what had happened.

In the meantime, they began their travels again. Both of them enjoyed the novels of Tolstoy and Dostoevsky and wanted to visit Russia at some point. Elisabeth studied Russian with an emigrée in order to read the novels in their own language, but it also came in very useful when in the July of that year they stepped aboard the luxurious and elegant Orient Express to take the journey from Paris to St Petersburg. Elisabeth was delighted that she could speak fluently to the Russian waiters on board in their own language.

They enjoyed the elegance of St Peterburg, but Elisabeth found the walking difficult. When they moved on to Moscow their mood changed. They were repulsed by the poverty, the dilapidated buildings and the hopelessness that they felt in the air; they enjoyed the beautiful churches with their brilliantly-coloured domes, but even Elisabeth felt that the expression of religion there of the people was more by rote than by conviction. They were not to know of the faith beneath the externals which would sustain the people when their faith was tested to the point of martyrdom and suppression with the October Revolution and the triumph of communism.

At this point, they already felt the oppression of it in the air, the presence of the secret police. They began to suffocate under it all and left without regrets to move on to the light and colour of Constantinople.

> The following year they journeyed to Tangier by way of Spain, and it was while journeying through the countryside perched on a mule that Elisabeth began to think deeply of how to proceed with developing her faith and reveal it to her husband. Silently she gave herself totally to God and realised that she had a calling to fulfil. Up until now, she felt her life had been empty and useless, but it 'will be transformed, I hope, by the strength of God and by close union with Him'.[15]

There were many souls around her, she wrote later of her meditations, and it was to them she was called to show the beauty of the Christian faith. She wanted to reach out 'with a lively sympathy' to everyone, 'and to do all this for God alone – that is the goal of all human existence'.

She returned home to resume her ordinary life but changed in herself. She knew she would need a great deal of courage to face the wrath of her husband, who would be furious when he realised that all his efforts had not resulted as he had planned. Elisabeth was determined that she would do everything to uphold their marriage, although that was never to be one-sided. There was a deep mutual love between them, and she would do nothing to change that. Elisabeth recognised that her husband, and no-one, would be changed by argument. She would build up her own faith within while remaining serene and untroubled by any attacks on it. By cultivating all that was best within herself, her God-given gifts, she could show to others the joy, the peace, the beauty of the Christian faith.

With her new-found faith came the need for a new lifestyle, in which she had to make time for prayer, reflection and reading. As a child and with her methodical mind, she had drawn up a daily timetable for herself, although then more in hope than in execution. She now did the same thing, so that her time would be used to the best advantage, but always with the flexibility her status in life demanded.

She found early on that the faith of her childhood and youth was insufficient to withstand the onslaught of atheism. She had to develop now the faith of an adult. Félix had built up a library of atheistic and anti-Catholic literature, Elisabeth now built up a library of Catholic writers from the Early Church Fathers and St Thomas Aquinas, for example, to contemporary theologians, that expressed the best of Catholicism. Her favourite author was St Francis de Sales, because his writings were addressed mainly to lay people rather than those in religious life. Elisabeth began to form for herself a lay spirituality that would draw on the best of mystical tradition, such as that of St Teresa of Avila and St Catherine of Siena, who became her two patrons. It was a well-balanced – and daunting – collection. In addition and above all, were the Scriptures, which became her daily reading and an unfailing source of light and strength.

When Félix realised that his plan had failed he was furious, especially when he had thought victory had been assured. He therefore redoubled his criticism, his scorn, his assaults on the Catholic Faith and the Church. Before, with both of them having, as they described it, 'a spirit of contradiction', with Félix in the first flush of his enthusiasm about atheism and with Elisabeth still retaining the faith of her upbringing, they would undoubtedly have had some lively but good-natured discussions. Now, Félix's attacks had a very different and bitter tone, as he tried at every turn to belittle and besmirch his wife's faith.

This meant that Elisabeth had to tread a difficult path, living with someone she loved deeply, but who not only failed to understand what was now most precious to her, but who was actively and resolutely opposed to it. It made in her a deep well of loneliness and isolation that could have been soul-sapping, but from which she had to make something positive. She had always kept a diary describing their travels and her reactions to the things she saw around her. Now, a year after her conversion she decided to keep a spiritual diary in which she could write about all the things that she could not express openly in any other way. She opened her diary 11 September 1899:

> For a year I have been thinking and praying a great deal; I have tried unceasingly to enlighten myself, and in this perpetual labour my mind has matured, my convictions have become more profound, and my love for souls has increased, too. What is there greater than the human soul, or finer than conviction?
>
> We must create in ourselves a 'new spirit', the spirit of intelligence and strength; we must renew ourselves and live our interior life with intensity. We must pray and act. Every day of our life must carry us nearer to the supreme Good and Intelligence – that is, nearer to God.[16]

This important entry maps out in embryo the pattern of her life from now on. She wanted, first of all, to understand another person's point of view, without in any way compromising her own beliefs, an outlook that had become fundamental to her through their travels. Through this way of understanding what motivated others and what was most dear to them she was able to broaden her horizons to a universal but never vague love. This was not easy, because she was surrounded by so much unbelief. Social evenings often became a time of great stress for her, when she had to listen to discussions that made a mockery of her faith. She wrote in her diary after one such occasion:

> Bitter suffering of an evening spent in hearing my faith and spiritual things mocked at, attacked and criticized. God helped me to maintain interior charity and exterior calm, to deny or betray nothing and yet not to irritate by too rigid assertions. But how much effort and interior distress this involves, and how necessary is divine grace to assist my weakness![17]

In addition, Félix would often arrange for the evening soirées in their home to take place on a Friday, so that Elisabeth would be obliged to provide a sumptuous meal, which would include meat, on the day in the week when Catholics traditionally observed abstinence in honour of the Lord's Passion and Death.

Elisabeth had to walk a fine line when taking in at a deep level what was being said in discussions, with which she might not agree, while at the same time retaining her own beliefs and being open to the other's point of view. She would strive to see the good and the true that it might contain:

> Not to accept everything, but to understand everything; not to approve of everything, but to forgive everything; not to adopt everything, but to search for the grain of truth that is contained in everything.[18]

Her friend, Aimée Fiévet, gave her impressions of Elisabeth during these social evenings:

> When she did not approve of a judgment, an idea expressed and she had reason to keep silent .... She neither protested by an expression on her face, nor by critique. From her silence emanated something inexpressible giving the impression that she had withdrawn into her soul, like putting something away in a safe place.

> She was a good listener, looking for the truth or wisdom of her interlocutor. If they did not come to agreement, she would end .... easily, with a smile full of resolve and hope and say, 'we will think about this each from our own side'.[19]

Elisabeth soon realised that argument would not convert anyone, and it was in any case not in her nature now to argue. She was deeply distressed when she saw how Jews were being treated in certain circles during the Dreyfuss affair, when, Dreyfuss, a Jewish officer in the army, was wrongly convicted of handing documents to the Germans. 'I wish I could organise a holy crusade against hate and promote justice among men and women', she wrote in her diary:

> Fanaticism fills me with horror, and I cannot understand how it can exist with sincere conviction. Can anyone who loves Christianity passionately and wishes to see it reign in souls think for one moment that he should use any method to achieve this goal other than persuasion? Can one instil conviction through force or deceit? Besides, is there not in the use of such means something completely repugnant to the upright loyal spirit that should mark every sincere Christian? And yet how many little acts of fanaticism we commit unconsciously?[20]

Elisabeth recognised that she had the ability to discern an 'intimate and personal action in the depths of the human soul and if she sensed that someone was more open to spiritual things she acted with discretion, knowing that the Lord has his own time, his own unique way of acting within the individual soul:

> In obliging me to live in the midst of total negation and indifference and that impenetrable ignorance of divine things that oppresses so many unfortunate people, He has doubtless intended that I should have compassion for, share myself with, and turn toward those who blaspheme and doubt with more pity and love.[21]

She would never compromise her own principles and beliefs but simply allow the other person to have the freedom to disagree, speaking of her own faith simply and clearly if she felt it was right to do so. She made an interesting observation that she was:

> Struck with the fact that unbelievers have more sympathy with people of deep faith than with those of variable and utilitarian views. These dear unbelievers attend more to those who are 'intransigent' regarding the Faith than to those who by subtlety and compromise hope to bring them to accept the Faith. And yet the bold statement must be made with the most intelligent sympathy and the liveliest and most delicate charity.[22]

Her daily prayer was for her beloved husband whom she knew would not be won over by argument or discussion, so deeply entrenched was his atheism. Therefore:

> Let him see the fruit but not the sap, my life but not the faith that transforms it, the light that is in me but not word of Him who brings it to my soul; let him see God without hearing His name.[23]

She wanted to be Christian to the very core of her being so that the whole of her life would speak of God:

> The adored Guest of my soul must be guessed at rather than plainly seen; every part of me must speak of Him without my saying His name; I must be an influence, without ever being a profession of faith.[24]

CHAPTER 4

WORK AMONG THE POOR

Elisabeth was amassing her library of spirituality, but it was not a spirituality that remained in her study. As a child, she mentioned in her diary that she had won a little bit of money in a game they were playing and noted that she had put it aside to give to the poor. This concern for the poor was fundamental to her nature and to her journey into ever deeper union with God. Her love would embrace the whole of humanity, but in her day to day living she would go out to one person at a time, whatever their condition, their religion or belief; indeed, she would go out specially to those who were most different from her, as she wrote in her diary:

> I want to love with a special love those whose birth or religion or ideas separate them from me; it is those especially whom I must try to understand and who need me to give them a little of what God has placed within me.[25]

Elisabeth's way was through love, prayer and example:

> To go more and more to souls, approaching them with respect and delicacy, touching them with love. To try always to understand everything and everyone. Not to argue; to work instead through contact and example; to dissipate prejudice, to reveal God and to make Him felt without speaking of Him.[26]

> Deep, unalterable respect for souls; never to do them violence, however gentle one tries to be, but to open wide one's soul to show the light in it and the truth that lives there, and to let that creative truth enlighten and transform, without any merit of our own, but simply by the fact of its presence in us.[27]

Elisabeth was saddened that among her own class and among many Catholics, there was very little interest or understanding about the needs that were on their very doorstep, although there were several eminent Catholics who were working on behalf of the poor, such as Montalembert, Albert de Mun and Goyau. She was equally scathing of the atheistic socialists and saw the limits of secular socialism, one of her maxims being, 'Socialism pretends to assure and transform the future; Christianity transforms the present'. She had no time for the various factions which were tearing each other apart with hatred for the other, while dreaming of establishing a universal brotherhood without first establishing that brotherhood within their own hearts.

'Politics deforms everything,' she wrote to Charles Duvent, an artist friend of hers. It was no point in dreaming of universal love tomorrow without trying to put it into practice today. One example of this woolly thinking was the Law of Associations the Government promulgated in 1902. While proclaiming their intention to provide full equality of secular education, free from ecclesiastical control, for both girls and boys, the Government succeeded in closing down more than 10,000 schools run by the Church through its religious Orders, without putting an equal alternative in its place. In the event, they had to re-open some 6,000 of them shortly afterwards, which were once again under religious control. Their vicious anti-clericalism drove them to try and abolish the very institutions that were providing the education that was needed. Elisabeth was, of course, completely supportive of the new move towards equal education for girls, while decrying its wholly secular ethos; for her, the most important task, the most urgent, was to reveal to people the idea of God.

She put her words into practice by setting up what she named 'Home for the Young Woman'. She recognised the need young women had for protection against the dangers of exploitation and prostitution in Paris, and in February 1903 rented a house in Vésinet. It was a large property set in a beautiful garden where the young girls could enjoy the peace and calm of their surroundings and learn dressmaking. They were required to pay a small monthly rent, since Elisabeth considered that things which were given for free were not appreciated. Sadly, due to lack of funds and support, she had to close it down.

Instead she had other organisations to which she committed herself, and which were totally in accord with her way of thought. One of these was the Union Populaire Catholique, set up by a remarkable woman, Mlle Muller, who had devoted her life to the poor. The work of the Union was organised on two principles, first, that one should be actively engaged in the work on a personal level, and the second was to encourage the people with whom they worked to come to a greater knowledge, love and commitment to God. The Union was active in the fauberges of Paris, among the most deprived and destitute, and was helping more than 2500 families. They helped the men to find work and ran training centres for them. They could be given help with their rent; the Union ran a furniture store, libraries, classes and adult catechism courses. It set up holiday camps for the children. On fixed days legal and medical centres would be open, with doctors and lawyers giving their time free of charge. Whatever need there was, the Union tried to give it. Each helper was assigned individual families to visit and thus build up a rapport with them to discern what their particular needs were, and the needs of the area. Some areas would have a dispensary, in another they would run a restaurant, or a garden providing work for the men.

Most importantly, the Union's aim was to bring the people back to God, and in this they had amazing success. Hundreds of children and adults were baptized, marriages performed or regularised, people brought back to the Faith. This was what appealed most to Elisabeth. She was assigned to a section of the Plaine-Saint-Denis, and she regularly visited the families assigned to her.

She often tried to enthuse Félix with what she was doing, but with little success. He was keen on the overseas missions, but to Elisabeth's eyes there was far more poverty, moral and physical misery which appalled her, at the gates of Paris, than they had ever seen in their travels abroad.

Elisabeth realised that people needed to be raised out of their poverty by decent work, education and better health, by giving them hope for the future, so that they could see themselves as treasured children of God created for eternal life with him. This was her vision, and she approached the families under her care with her habitual delicacy, sensitivity and innate charm, embodying in herself what she was trying to bring to them for themselves.

Elisabeth was also closely involved in another, very similar organisation, the Union Familiale, set up in the Charonne quarter, one of the most deprived areas of Paris, by another woman of exceptional charity, Mlle Gahéry, described as having a strong will and outstanding intelligence, just the sort of person to whom Elisabeth would be drawn. Again, the Union was all-embracing in what it offered to the working men and women of the area. It set up classes for the young people and children, including summer camps, it taught them management skills and gave teacher training. The emphasis was on education – the women in household skills, young people on schooling, the men in best work practices.

Elisabeth worked with the smallest children, especially here, a work that so suited her maternal nature. Because of her medical condition and to her great sorrow she was unable to have children herself, she lavished her love on these little ones and was loved by them in return.

She spoke of the work with enthusiasm to an uninterested Félix, but she was eventually able to persuade him to come with her and see for himself the work that was being done. It was not a success; Félix saw Elisabeth's delight as she took him round and showed him everything. He saw the very real love she had for the children and the genuine affection and love they had for her, the influence she had over them by her calm and gentle firmness. In the restaurant they ate cakes that had been made in the catering school. But the poverty of the people, the barrenness of the surroundings, repelled him and he just could not understand the goodness and enthusiasm that Elisabeth visibly radiated. As they left, she asked Félix what his impressions were, and he responded with a grimace of disgust, remarking that 'Frankly, you know, I would prefer to go to the Rothschilds!'

Elisabeth smiled sadly, disheartened by Félix's response, but in her habitual gentle way replied, 'Don't say that. Suffering is the only thing of value here below; the day will come when the light will shine for you and you will understand. I pray daily that God will give you that grace'.

Charles Duvent, on the other hand, who was also involved in social concerns, had a great respect for Elisabeth and what he saw as her optimism, but she was quick to place the credit for this where it was due:

> You speak of my optimism, and what you call such is made
> up for me of many rough patches, great and small, of sacrifices

and sadnesses; I well believe this name does not suit the condition you mean by it. Only – and I say this very humbly, because it is no merit of mine, but a grace – I have a very great and very precious resource ... I console myself with the God of humanity and I return a little better and soothed about poor humans, my brothers.

That is why, my dear friend, sorrowful as I so often am, like you, in this contact with the realities of life I cannot become bitter and scornful.[28]

Not that Elisabeth found it easy to walk among the ugliness of poverty, something that Duvent the artist appreciated. Writing to him Elisabeth brought up this aspect of her work:

Yes, there is much evil, much meanness in the world, and the great error of the socialists and other reformers is to imagine that through violence, through the theories they develop, humanity will discover how to regenerate itself and enter into an era of endless happiness.[29]

She makes here the important point that true reform can never come through violence or be imposed from the outside. She herself could have fallen into the trap of coming in to the situation as a 'do-gooder', imposing her own ideas. As always, Elisabeth was acutely aware of the other person, no matter how poor, who had a dignity and a worth of their own, in whom God's grace was working; her role was to act as a catalyst if necessary, but above all being, herself, the best that she could be. In her letter to Charles, she continues:

My dear friend, I am starting from a different point of view. I am persuaded that evil and suffering will never completely desert our poor earth, but I am also convinced that it is everyone's task to work to reduce evil and suffering as much as possible, in our own sphere, humbly, simply, without concern for our precious personality, through dedication, love, the gift of ourselves to that which is our duty.[30]

It was difficult for Elisabeth to move from this work among the poorest to the circles where she and Félix would be completely at home calling on the Rothschilds. There she found a different sort of poverty, a poverty of spirit, of shallowness and what she called frivolity. She saw them as children, equally in need of her love:

> I must nevertheless know how to make myself all things to all men and interest myself in things that sometimes seem childish, and which sadden me by their contrast with my own state of mind. Often people are like great children, but Jesus has said that what is done for children is done for Him. Has not God done the same with us, and has He not placed in our souls only as much light as we can bear?[31]

CHAPTER 5

INNER LIFE

One year, some close friends, the Hennequins, invited the Leseurs to their holiday home in Jougne, high in the French alps by the French Swiss border. Elisabeth and Félix so fell in love with the little village that they had a holiday home built there themselves, and it became a much-loved home for all the extended family. Elisabeth always preferred the country, where she could rest and recuperate, to the noise and stresses of Paris.

She loved being surrounded by her nephews and niece, friends and family in Jougne. The children knew not to disturb 'Aunt Bébeth' from 10 o'clock for a while, because this was a time she kept for her time of prayer. Then she would join the rest of the family on the terrace, relaxing on a chaise longue, joining in the chat and writing long letters to her wide circle of friends.

She was a delightful companion. One of her favourite saints was St Teresa of Avila, whom she loved not only for her spiritual writings but also because Teresa had no time for sad saints. However difficult Elisabeth was finding her various trials she did not allow them to be visible to others, writing:

> To smile and share in the joys and pleasures of others when the body is overcome with fatigue is better than to give oneself in good health, for the effort is greater. May others see in me only that which can bring them comfort or do them some good, and may Thee alone, my God, know the silent battles in my will and heart.[32]

She needed the rest and relaxation Jougne gave her because her health was continuing to deteriorate. In 1901 she developed liver problems on top of everything else. It was also not helped by an accident she had had years earlier, when the coach they were travelling in overturned and the horse kicked in her side, leaving her bedbound for several months.

Now, she was often confined to bed with pain and fever and began to realise that she had to start reducing her active work, writing in her diary that 'more and more I see that God does not want me to be active unless a new state of affairs should arise'. She longed to be an apostle but realised that her apostolate would from now on be more and more that of prayer, united with suffering, and the two would be inseparable.

Elisabeth radiated a quiet tranquillity, regardless of her inner struggles. Yvonne, a childhood friend, often became upset and worried, and her husband's advice was to 'go and visit Elisabeth and take a bath in her serenity'. This serenity flowed from her increasingly profound union with God. In a little 'treatise' she wrote for her niece Marie, she wrote of those friends of hers with whom she worked in Paris, but which so well described her own self:

> They are rare, no doubt, but there flows from them such an intensity of inner life, such calm strength, such true beauty that merely to come into contact with them soothes and comforts us. After all, this is only natural. Our outer life is the reproduction of our inner life, and the visible part of us reflects what is unseen; we radiate our souls, so to speak, and, when they are centres of light and warmth, other souls need only to be brought into contact with them in order to be warmed and enlightened. We give out, often unknown to ourselves, what we carry within us; let us strive to increase daily this reserve store of faith and quiet charity.[33]

Her atheist friend Aimée thought that Elisabeth was placing something in her Catholic faith that wasn't really there, but Elisabeth strongly disagreed. She said that the Faith, its sacraments, the Scriptures, its dogmas and liturgies, were like a stained-glass window in a cathedral. From the outside it looked dead and leaden. Only from the inside did it reveal its true glory and light. Elisabeth lived deep within her Catholic faith; it was her spiritual lifeblood, her home, nourishing her at her deepest level. She wrote often of how the sacrament of Confession, receiving Holy Communion at Mass, gave her peace and renewal when her spirits flagged. The Scriptures and the writings of the saints and spiritual writers down the ages fed her mind and heart. The Church's 'dogmas', its teachings, handed on down the ages in the commission given to her by Christ himself to teach all nations, were her anchor. She loved following the Church's liturgy through the year, with its great feasts and the birthdays into heaven of the saints in an unending procession, connected her to her brothers and sisters in the Faith:

> Catholic liturgy has a great charm for me; I love to live, in the course of the year, the great collective life of the Church, uniting myself with its joys and sorrows, joining my feeble prayers, my weak voice, with its powerful voice... to feel myself a living cell in the great Catholic union; and to come, after so many others, and before so many others who follow me with my homage to the infant God, the suffering Christ, the risen Lord.[34]

In this excerpt she gives her understanding of a dogma that meant a great deal to her: the Communion of Saints. She recognised that she was united with all those who had gone before her, the saints known and unknown, including her beloved relatives. Their prayers helped her on her journey, her prayer was united with theirs in that great 'treasury' of prayer and holiness that stretched out from the past, to the present and beyond, into the future, because, being in God, they were beyond the limits of time and space.

Her work among the poor also was all part of her profound belief in the Communion of Saints, where every action, even the smallest and most hidden, when done in love, has eternal repercussions, saying, 'one act of goodness raises the whole world'. Also, when her health began to give way and she was less and less able to take on active work, she had the vivid assurance that her prayer, her suffering, was of immense value for those whom she sought to serve. She would still have her apostolate, but in a different form. Nothing is wasted in the eyes of God.

In 1903 the Leseurs went to Rome for Holy Week with the Hennequins; it was here that Elisabeth had one of her profound moments of union with God which grounded her even more deeply into his love:

> I felt in myself the living presence of the blessed Christ, of God Himself, bringing me an ineffable love; this incomparable Soul spoke to mine, and all the infinite tenderness of the Saviour passed for an instant into me. Never will this divine

trace be effaced. The triumphant Christ, the Eternal Word, He who as man has suffered and loved, the one living God, took possession of my soul for all eternity in that unforgettable moment. I felt myself renewed to my very depths by Him, ready for a new life, for duty, for the work intended by His Providence. I give myself without reserve, and I give Him the future.[35]

Elisabeth's peace and her belief in the Communion of Saints received its cruellest test but also rooted her more profoundly in its truth, when her beloved sister, Juliette, to whom Elisabeth had been like a little mother when they were children, became terminally ill with tuberculosis. Elisabeth said Juliette, who had never married, was her best self, and there was a sweetness and a most attractive gentleness about her, combined with an excellent mind and intelligence.

During her sister's final weeks Elisabeth spent as much time with her as she could, and a deep spiritual bond united them. When she died, 13 April 1905, Elisabeth could only note that date in her diary, with a cross, only in July able to put her grief into words in her diary.

Juliette's death made her even more convinced of the truth of the Communion of Saints, that, despite the sorrow of her no longer being with them, Juliette was living now an even richer life in heaven:

Oh, I cannot believe that my constant ardent prayers, and those of others for her, and all the sacrifices offered and the tears shed, and so much suffering accepted, could all be useless. I do not believe that all her trials, her life of privation and grief ended by a sweet and holy death could be without fruit.

If earthly happiness was denied her, if she knew bitter and sad separations, and if in the end she was taken from us, it is that a better life awaited her than on this earth, it is that joy out of all comparison with her cruel suffering was prepared for her by the God of love, and that God wished her to know all beauty and all good and to give her His light, and that her dear soul was purified and holy enough to enter into the domain of sanctity.[36]

Coping with her own ill health, entering ever more deeply into the life of God in prayer, her greatest privation now Juliette was no longer with her, was 'the absence of any deep, long, Christian conversation' with some like-minded friend, something she thought she would never happen to her. There is a difference between solitude and isolation:

> I love interior solitude with God alone; it strengthens my soul, and gives it light and fervour again. But sometimes isolation, which is a different thing entirely from solitude, weighs it down.[37]

However, God was soon to give her the great blessing of one whom she called her 'soul sister'.

CHAPER 7

FINAL DAYS

On their way to Jougne in 1910, the Leseurs made a detour to visit the famous Hôtel Dieu in Beaune, the magnificent hospital that served the terminally ill. Elisabeth stopped by the bed of a little girl, Marie Ballard, who was dying of tuberculosis and chatted with her. She asked Marie if there was anything she would like, and the little girl asked her for a coloured postcard. Telling her nurse later of the lovely lady who had stopped to speak to her, the nurse, Sr Goby, warned the child not to raise her hopes too much; she knew from experience that many visitors made promises but forgot them as soon as they had left. Elisabeth, however, was no ordinary visitor, and from the next town they stopped at she sent Marie a lovely postcard, with more to come. Sr Goby, on behalf of little Marie, wrote to Elisabeth to thank her:

> Madame,
>
> I do not have the honour of knowing you, and yet allow me to join my respectful thanks to those of my dear little invalid. I was profoundly touched by your delicate charity towards that poor little child. Your lovely cards are for her a ray of sunshine; I assure you that on receiving them, I saw a smile dawn on her young face which usually bore the imprint of sadness and suffering, and I myself was happy and ask God to repay such delicate goodness.[38]

This was followed later by a doll that Marie said she would love, a beautiful doll that far surpassed her expectations; sadly, she died later that year, but her last months had been made happy by Elisabeth's generosity. The Leseurs continued to send generous gifts to the hospital and kept up their association with it.

While Sr Goby wrote on Marie's behalf to thank Elisabeth for the gifts, gradually their correspondence became less formal and more that of friends who shared the same hunger for holiness. God had given to them the 'soul friend' they had both longed for.

The following year the Leseurs once more visited Beaune, and Sr Goby and Elisabeth were able to meet each other for the first time. Elisabeth first attended the Mass in the chapel, and Sr Goby had no difficulty in recognising her among the other visitors. In a letter to Elisabeth later she gives a glimpse of the effect Elisabeth had on her; it was an impression others would also surely have experienced:

> I had seen the radiance of that same spirit on your face when I saw you near the tabernacle of our little chapel when I approached you for the first time!
>
> I found it again shining through the features of your face and expressing itself in our conversation in our intimate hour in the morning! And then, oh! instantly I loved you and felt so attracted to you! Yes, I want my soul to become a true Sister to yours.[39]

Elisabeth had need of Sr Goby's prayers and support, because the previous year she had been worried about a small tumour on her breast, which turned out to be cancerous. On Palm Sunday 1911 she entered a small hospital which had been a Carmelite monastery, from which the monks had been expelled under the Law of Associations. She had the operation the following day and Félix nursed her tenderly through the painful aftermath. For Elisabeth, there was the great blessing of a chapel still attached to the hospital where she could attend Mass; both enjoyed the serene surroundings and the peace that still lingered there. It was a time for blessing for them both, and their love for each other grew even deeper. That tender, mutual love was most beautifully expressed in a letter Elisabeth wrote shortly afterwards:

> It is you, my dear Félix, who will be the first recipient of lines written by me after that operation. I would want them to be able to express my profound tenderness and that gratitude of the very sweet burden borne during those days of trial; my patron, St Elizabeth, changed humble bread into roses; you found ways of transforming into joys and consolations the most intimate and very profound sufferings. In my helplessness I loved you even more; where I pay you my debt of gratitude,

I confide to God that dear belief. Better than I can, he will repay you a hundredfold what you have given to me and what you have done for me – My beloved, I embrace you with all my tenderness.

Your wife

Elisabeth[40]

The operation was a success and Elisabeth was able for a time to resume some of her previous activities. When she was unable to take an active part in the various associations, she served as their secretary. She longed more and more for solitude, but smilingly donned the furs and dresses required by her status for the social events they attended. Years before, though, she had decided to simplify her clothing, without making them unsuitable for the occasion and always expressing her natural flair and elegance. All her outward activity now flowed from her inner union with God and gave them purpose:

> People in the world do not realise that one can be very detached from all human things and live a keen spiritual life, and yet find sweetness in the interests, occupations, and joys of life. However, it is only when one has rooted oneself in eternity that one can let one's humble little barque float upon the surface of the waves and rejoice fully in the view from earthly rivers.[41]

During Easter 1912, she noted in her diary that she wanted 'to become both more "interior" and more "exterior", however paradoxical that may seem':

> My soul should live in a more complete, intimate union with God; prayer should be the foundation of my spiritual life, my surest means of apostolate, my best form of charity; my suffering, with my habitual or voluntary mortifications, will also be the means I will take for doing good to souls and drawing near to the heart of God.

> But exteriorly I will make myself, through divine grace, more gentle, more loving, occupied always and exclusively for others, their pleasure, their good, and above all, their souls. This in all humility, effacing myself, and making of my entire

spiritual life a life hidden in God.[42]

Gradually her health declined, despite her best efforts to conceal it, and she was more and more bedridden. Having trained as a doctor, Félix was well aware that patients who suffered from the liver disease from which his wife was also suffering, caused them to become very impatient and irascible. He could only marvel, then, at his wife's almost unfailing patience and serenity; he could see that such joy in the midst of such suffering came from her faith, and he found his opposition to it softening a little.

There were periods of better health when she could take walks in the nearby Bois de Boulogne. From a holiday in Jougne she wrote to Sr Goby:

> Let us abandon ourselves to him, and through all aridity, sadness of soul, through all the pains of heart and of life, through all bodily suffering, let us march towards the divine Light, which hides itself here below only in order to give us greater light above. Let us wrap ourselves in serenity, let us spend ourselves lavishly in charity, and let us be by prayer and sorrow apostles of Jesus. It is a beautiful programme; you will accomplish it more quickly than I.[43]

She felt keenly her bodily fatigue, the pain, the humiliations that her illnesses brought, the spiritual dryness, but found that all her exterior circumstances could not overwhelm her deep inner peace:

> May God be praised for all joys and griefs. May He help me, by the spiritual joy that exists even in the midst of interior gloom, to praise and glorify Him until I breathe no more, until I enter eternity.[44]

She longed to be an apostle, and she was now living her new apostolate, that of prayer and suffering in the heart of the Church for souls. Her longing for more solitude in which she could unite herself ever more closely to God, was fulfilled in her sickroom.

Tuesday, 28 April, a priest came to give her extreme unction. The following day, as so often happens after receiving the sacrament, she rallied a little and had a last period of lucidity. She gave her beloved husband one last smile of such love and tenderness that it nearly broke his heart. She then slipped into a period of agonising fever and thirst, which they tried to alleviate by wetting her lips with a water-filled sponge. Finally, at 10 o'clock in the morning, Sunday 3 May 1914, in the arms of her husband, she gently gave up her soul to the God whom she had loved so passionately here on earth.

CHAPTER SIX

FROM ATHEIST TO PRIEST

Félix was devasted at his loss, but marvelled at the serenity, almost an aura, that remained on Elisabeth's face after death. In his diary he wrote:

> She has been installed on her deathbed, and the expression of suffering that she had in the morning has been succeeded by a ravishing expression of bliss, an exquisite smile. A gentle vision and very consoling to retain.[45]

The 'look of immortal beauty', as he also described it – he, who did not believe in immortality! - Elisabeth's face bearing the calm of another world, moved him deeply. At her funeral he was amazed at the number of people, often poor people, who attended the Mass; many of the people he had never known and would never see again, but whose lives Elisabeth had touched in so many ways.

In the days that followed, to fill the immense void left in his life and encouraged by Amélie, who knew of its existence, he found Elisabeth's diary and began to read it. It completely overwhelmed him. He read there of the immense love his wife had had for him, the prayer and suffering she had offered for him over the years, the faith that meant all the world to her and which he had so derided. He was overcome with remorse.

As the days passed he felt himself guided by Elisabeth herself, drawing him gently but firmly into her own world vision of the reality of God's existence, against all his natural inclinations as an atheist. Thinking about the love that had radiated from her, her inner beauty, the intelligence, the nobility of her character, be began to wonder whether such characteristics could simply cease to exist after death.

A friend, to take him out of his isolation, proposed that they went on a trip together, and as they were driving through the beautiful French countryside, out of the blue Félix heard Elisabeth's voice, as clearly as he had heard it before her death, in a phrase she had used then, saying 'I am grieved'. Over the days and weeks that followed he heard that voice again, gently guiding him, while his work and his milieu often drew him back into his accustomed atheism.

Then the First World War intervened. As the people began to flee Paris ahead of the expected German invasion, Félix was charged with taking the firm's assets to the relative safety of Bordeaux. He managed to share a car with a friend as far as Vierzon, and then he boarded a crowded train for the final leg of the journey. Sitting on the precious portmanteau in the luggage van, the only space left for him, exhausted yet grateful for how things had worked out for him, he once again heard Elisabeth's voice:

> You were able to leave Paris in a most unexpected, almost miraculous manner, but do not think that this was simply in order to safeguard the material interests entrusted to your care. That was only incidental: the true reason and aim of all this is your innermost being, which is here in question; it was necessary that you should be enabled to go to Lourdes, where God is awaiting you; Lourdes is the real object of your present journey. Go to Lourdes.[46]

Having delivered the portmanteau in Bordeaux and having rested with friends, Félix felt himself refreshed enough to make that fateful journey to Lourdes.

The town was much changed from his previous visits because very few pilgrims were there, with no processions or crowds. Instead, the hospices had been put at the disposal of the military to nurse the wounded. Lourdes was changed for Félix internally, too; he recalled the first time he had come and had despised what he had perceived as the superstition and commercialisation, the 'gullibility' and what he was sure were the 'fraudulent cures'. But he also recalled how at their last visit he had seen Elisabeth praying at the grotto, almost in ecstasy, and it was her spirit, above all, that was with him now.

Every morning he made his way to the Grotto and dropped to his knees, hardly knowing how to pray, but knowing only he wanted the gift of faith. Gradually he felt his heart changing:

Now my eyes were being opened, and I began to perceive that the Grotto of Massabielle is a sacred place, where God does indeed reveal Himself, and grace flows abundantly. I felt at peace within myself, and my sorrow began to assume a fresh meaning, in accordance with Elisabeth's profound words: 'Suffering gives birth to life'. I thanked God with all my heart. Of course, my faith was not yet self-conscious and reasoned, but henceforth I felt myself turning towards it, and was sure that I should find it and enter upon a new existence.[47]

The place that he had once so despised as full of superstition and gullibility was now to be the place of his conversion. With a divine sense of humour God was guiding him back to the Church by the very things that he had derided for so long. Félix was being drawn back, not by intellectual argument or study but by the spirituality and faith that spoke to the heart.

He returned to Paris transformed, and began to read books from Elisabeth's library, which gave substance to his new-found faith. The next step was to go to Confession to be reconciled to God and the Church; a friend made an appointment for him to see a Dominican priest, Fr Hébert, who had been Elisabeth's own confessor and spiritual director; the priest heard his confession and told him, to his amazement, to go to Mass and receive Holy Communion the following day.

Before she died, Elisabeth had received an inner assurance that Felix would return to the Church. More remarkably, she also received the conviction that he would also become a Dominican and a priest. This now happened, against the wishes of his family, who perhaps understandably felt it was unwise for him to make such a decision so soon after his conversion. Also, he had long been used to the fine wines and dining and the comforts of his home; he was 58 years old and it would be a difficult transition to embrace the austerities of the religious life, but Félix was driven by a true sense of vocation. He even went with Fr Hébert to Rome to seek the Pope's permission, something the Pope was at first reluctant to give, until he saw the depths of Félix's determination.

He entered the Dominican novitiate in 1919. Most of the novices with him were young men who had recently returned from the front. Félix thought that he might be out of place with them, but instead they greatly appreciated his wisdom, his good humour and his kindly nature. He brought to the Order a lifetime of culture and learning.

On 8 July 1923 he was ordained to the priesthood. He said his first Mass in the crypt of the Dominican convent in the faubourg Saint-Honoré. He could not help but recall that it was the same church, twenty years before, in which Elisabeth had stood as sponsor to a young man, one of his employees, who was being received into the Church. Then, Félix had been amused and incredulous that a grown man would voluntarily take such a step. Now, a Dominican and a priest, he recalled that this was what Elisabeth had foretold, and felt her presence very close to him.

In his priestly life, Félix made it his mission to spread knowledge of Elisabeth's life and spirituality. He had already overseen the publication of her diary and written a biography of her. He went on preaching tours and replied personally to the flood of letters that began to pour in from all over the world, speaking of cures that had occurred due to her intercession and the impact her life and spirituality had had on them. He began amassing the enormous amount of documentation that would be needed to advance the cause of her beatification and canonisation. Sadly, all this came to nothing with the onset of the Second World War. Félix had to accept that despite all his efforts and with his failing health he could do no more and had to leave it in the hands of God. He died 27 February 1950.

The influence that Elisabeth's writings and the example of her life never went away. Her 'Secret Diary' has never been out of print, in many languages, and now her Cause has once more been taken up by the Dominican Order. May Elisabeth continue to be a holy guide to those who are battling with illness, to see its value allied with prayer when united with the redemptive suffering of Christ. May her serenity and delicate, discerning charity be an example to those living or working in an environment hostile to Christianity. May she be an advocate for those who are unable to have children and yet can make the maternal instinct fruitful in the service of others. May she encourage us to deepen our understanding of the faith through study and contemplation. May she show us how to work for our community, for the poor in material or spiritual things, showing forth the compassion of Christ, being a radiant and joyful witness to Christ in us, to God's greater glory.

Elisabeth and Félix Leseur

Elisabeth at her writing desk

PART TWO

THE ADORED GUEST OF MY SOUL

In her 'secret diary' and other notebooks, Elisabeth Leseur wrote of her often lonely struggles to grow in her faith surrounded by an active atheism that was determined to undermine it. Her husband, throughout their marriage, was unable to understand why her faith meant so much to her, and, even more importantly, the depths of it within her soul. It was the wellspring of all that she did in her life, from her work among the poor of Paris, to studying the political changes that were taking place in France and in the world, to continuing to nourish her soul with reading the great classics of Catholic spirituality and theology and her life of prayer. In all that she did, she wanted to 'become Christian to the core'.

Elisabeth realised that she could withstand the challenge of a milieu empty of God only by being fully immersed in her own faith and, when she discerned it to be timely, helping to bring others to faith, too. Prayer was her greatest weapon and the means by which she deepened her union with her greatest love, Jesus. For her, from the time of her conversion, it was prayer united with suffering – physical suffering which gradually increased for her, the mockery and distain directed at what was most precious to her, the mental suffering of loneliness and isolation in those times when she had no-one with whom she could share the deepest impulses of her soul. She was to find, though, a deep well of happiness and joy that sustained her and brought her close to heaven even in this life.

In the following pages we will follow Elisabeth in her hidden journey of faith and love, a journey that began for her already on earth and was fulfilled completely for her in heaven:

I thirst for life, the only Life, full and eternal, with all our affections recovered in the bosom of Infinite Love. [48]

MEETING ATHEISM

When on that day in 1898, Elisabeth asked Félix for something to read and he gave her the works of Auguste Renan, it began for Elisabeth a journey of faith towards the most intense union with God. Elisabeth found it difficult to be among their acquaintances and friends hearing the faith that now meant so much to her, mocked and dismissed:

> Bitter suffering of an evening spent in hearing my faith and spiritual things mocked at, attacked, and criticized. God helped me to maintain interior charity and exterior calm; to deny or betray nothing, and yet not to irritate by too rigid assertions. But how much effort and interior distress this involves, and how necessary is divine grace to assist my weakness![49]

To maintain her Christian faith in such surroundings would not be easy. Elisabeth recognized that she would need courage, resilience. She resolved to maintain interior and exterior serenity, that would at the same time enable her to keep close to her divine Guest within, while showing to others, in the peace and joy that she genuinely possessed, the fruit and the beauty of the Christian faith:

> Many of them do not know God or know Him only imperfectly. It is not in arguing or in lecturing that I can make them know what God is to the human soul. But in struggling with myself, in becoming, with His help, more Christian and more valiant, I will bear witness to Him whose humble disciple I am. By the serenity and strength that I mean to acquire I will prove that the Christian life is great and beautiful and full of joy. By cultivating all the best faculties of my mind I will

proclaim that God is the highest Intelligence and that those who serve Him can draw without end from that blessed source of intellectual and moral light.[50]

In seeing in God the 'highest Intelligence', she was refuting the perception of atheists that believers were stupid and ignorant. Elisabeth herself was an outstanding example of one who was continually studying her faith, drawing on some of the greatest minds that had ever lived, such as St Augustine and St Thomas Aquinas, so that, in the words of St Peter, she should 'always have your answer ready for people who ask you the reason for the hope that you all have. But give it with courtesy and respect and with a clear conscience... (1 Peter 3: 15-16)

She would not retaliate in kind to so much mockery, but with love:

In obliging me to live in the midst of total negation and indifference and that impenetrable ignorance of divine things that oppresses so many unfortunate people, He has doubtless intended that I should have compassion for, share myself with, and turn toward those who blaspheme and doubt with more pity and love.[51]

Among their close friends was Félix le Dantec, husband of her childhood friend, Yvonne. Although a convinced atheist, Elisabeth recognised his integrity and the nobility of his character, while he acknowledged her as being 'at the peak of humanity'. They had some lively discussions, but as so often, Elisabeth found that the arguments of atheists failed to convince because they did not correspond to the lived belief of a Christian:

You want to convince us of our absurdity through arguments that do not convince us, because we will be able to respond that whereas you argue in order to persuade us that we are unreasonable, we 'live' from a higher life, entirely interior, so penetrated with faith that our moral being is transformed by it and that at the same time we are able to remain very humble, since we feel that this life has been given to us and that we do not believe this on our own.[52]

Elisabeth soon realised that argument was futile, but she wanted to understand deeply the other person's point of view, recognising that God had put the spark of his life into everyone; she wanted to find that grain of truth even in that which was most opposed to her own beliefs, without compromising herself:

Not to accept everything, but to understand everything; not to approve of everything, but to forgive everything; not to adopt everything, but to search for the grain of truth that is contained in everything.[53]

This involved real inner and spiritual hardship, but even this can be used by God. Elisabeth began to realise that God had put her into this particular situation for a purpose. Her own inner strength began to develop, and she wanted to have a deep understanding, too, of those who thought and believed so differently to her:

It is the time for painful effort: one must tear oneself asunder, forsake the realm of thought for that of reality, face action, know that one will either not be understood or be understood wrongly, and that one will perhaps suffer at the hands of humanity for having willed the good of humanity. We must already have drawn from God an incomparable strength and armed our hearts with patience and love, in order to undertake day by day and hour by hour the work that should belong to every Christian: the moral and material salvation of his brothers.[54]

Witnessing in the World

In a 'little treatise' she wrote for her young nephew, André, she spoke of the difficulties he would face as he went to work in the world, and the courage he would need to remain firm and constant in his faith. She spoke from her own bitter experience of being met with disdain, with sarcasm:

> You will have to struggle, in the first place, against the world, evil suggestions, bad companions, and a terrible thing that few can withstand: sarcasm. To be able to stand firm in spite of a disdainful smile is a token of perfect moral strength. For you, dear child, I dread a companion who makes fun of you, more than one who makes a brutal attack upon you; the latter will disgust you, but the former will disturb your peace of mind, and this disturbance is often the first sign of weakening.[55]

Christians might try to water down their faith in order to accommodate themselves to other beliefs, but Elisabeth discovered that this wasn't really the best path. She was:

> Struck with the fact that unbelievers have more sympathy with people of deep faith than with those of variable and utilitarian views. These dear unbelievers attend more to those who are 'intransigent' regarding the Faith than to those who by subtlety and compromise hope to bring them to accept the Faith. And yet the bold statement must be made with the most intelligent sympathy and the liveliest and most delicate charity.[56]

A Witness to Catholic Unity and Faith

She understood how people could be put off the Catholic Faith, seeing it only from the outside. From the inside, Elisabeth could only admire and love what she saw. Responding to her friend Aimée's objections, she wrote:

If you had, my friend, once studied thoroughly the structure of the Christian faith without any preconceived antipathy, you would at least be able to recognise how it all fits together so well, so solid, and how many different parts are connected one to another to the point of touching upon parts of the building could crumble were one to take a part out. Thus, in the whole building there is an admirable solidity. But I understand that one must admit the bases and that faith is the foundation of everything. I have only wanted to defend in the presence of your loyal spirit a great thing that we contemplate from two different perspectives. When you see the exterior windows of a church, you see only some unformed fragments, but from the inside, it is colourful and harmonious. Thus we both see something different at the same time.[57]

A visit to Rome in April 1903, and her sight of Pope Leo XIII, gave her a profound insight into this unity of the Church, not only in her teaching but also in her members:

I recall that almost transparent old man, clothed in white, with lively but profound eyes, with a noble gesture, his long transparent hand raised in blessing; the acclamation of the crowd, and I experience once more the overwhelming sense I had at that moment. An inner happiness, an inexpressible sweetness, and I felt myself a member of that great living body which is the Church, of being united as one in that vast community, and a participation in that life which circulates in Christianity and, because of him, united in one same love, not only for those, like me, who are a part of the body of the Church, but of all those souls of good will.[58]

However, she was willing to deprive herself of that which most fed her interior life – Mass and Holy Communion – if she felt that receiving it often would give rise to gossip:

Holy Communion is a happiness that I would give myself more often if it were not my duty to deprive myself of it sometimes, in order to avoid offending prejudice. The strength God brings to the soul, the sweetness of His presence, the vitality communicated by that blessed contact with Him can neither be described nor explained. To those who marvel at this miracle of divine love one can only say: 'Taste and see'.[59]

Elisabeth had a delicate sense of discernment and was generous with her time, giving books freely to people if she thought it would help, but she realised that her own life had to speak most clearly, transformed as it was through the grace of God given to her. 'To sum up', she wrote in her diary:

To reserve for God alone the depths of my soul and my interior life as a Christian. To give to others serenity, charm, kindness, useful words and deeds. To make Christian truth loved through me, but to speak of it only as an explicit demand or a need so clear as to seem truly providential. To preach by prayer, sacrifice, and example.[60]

The adored Guest of my soul must be guessed at rather than plainly seen; every part of me must speak of Him without me saying His name; I must be an influence, without ever being a profession of faith.[61]

As she wrote concerning her relationship with her husband, but which she always applied to others:

…to be extremely reserved concerning matters of faith, which are still veiled to him. If a quiet statement should sometimes be necessary, or if I can fruitfully show him a little of what is in my heart, that must at least be a rare event, done after careful thought, performed in all gentleness and sincerity.

46

Let him see the fruit but not the sap, my life but not the faith that transforms it, the light that is in me but not a word of Him who brings it to my soul; let him see God without hearing His name.[62]

LIVING THE CHRISTIAN LIFE IN THE WORLD

The Leseurs were very wealthy and moved among the upper echelons of Parisian society. Elisabeth therefore, had to plan her days to enable her to live an intense life of union with God, at the same time fulfilling all the obligations of her state:

> The milieu in which I live, certain people's hostility, the variety and sometimes the complication of my duties, the influence I can have on the hearts who love my own heart and on the spirits who come to me with confidence, all demand great circumspection from me. If I must be so exact in not to neglect the smallest detail of my rule when I alone am concerned, it would not do to act in the same way when a neighbour is in question. My resolutions should therefore be adaptable to circumstances. The precept of charity should come before any measure intended to ensure the solidity and intensity of my spiritual life.[63]

> I occupy myself with clothes and furs… and talk about them, so as to give no hint of austerities. How afraid the world is of suffering and penance, and how carefully I must hide both of these, as much as possible, from the eyes of my neighbour! My friendliness and charity will with God's help draw hearts to Him who is so good.[64]

For Christians, it can be difficult to walk the tightrope, as it were, of being in the world with all its challenges and problems, while at the same time maintaining their inner life of faith. It is the challenge of combining Martha and Mary. But faith can so inform the life of a Christian as to give it a divine dimension:

Martha and Mary! The eternal conflict of material life and external existence with the imperishable needs of the soul, the call from without, pressing us to uncover the hidden forces of our soul, to abandon inner recollectedness for the activity that is more pure, more fruitful, or so it seems. But the Master has answered the question and ended the conflict. Mary triumphs; and if our bodies must often be given to the humble tasks of Martha, it is only on condition that our soul, like Mary, devotes itself to the contemplation and adoration of Him who speaks the divine word, and that we know how to listen in silence to that word in the depths of ourselves. The worth of activity lies only in the meditation that has prepared it and in the offering of it to God.[65]

She realised that with her work among the poor, running her household, fulfilling her social obligations, could lead to a chaotic life, so Elisabeth made a plan for daily activities, mapping out her day as far as possible, allowing for the unexpected, putting charity and making time to be with God at the head of everything. She gave advice to Emilie Alcan, because such advice was useful, whether a believer or unbeliever. We also have to say 'no' sometimes!

We must decide clearly what our real duties are, and here there are two pitfalls to be avoided. We must not be too ready to imagine that certain so-called obligations are really binding upon us, or we shall allow ourselves to be worried and distracted by a multitude of useless trifles; nor, on the other hand, must we neglect what are real duties, from which nothing can dispense us. We should carefully arrange our duties in order, never letting those of lowest rank encroach upon the more important. Highest of all stands moral duty, and if I give it precedence over the rest, it is because it includes them all, and because the way in which we discharge our other duties will depend upon the way in which we fulfil and understand this one.[66]

I have ordered all my days so that as much as possible they may represent, as it were, the whole of my life in miniature. Prayer, my precious morning meditation, work seriously performed, some work or care for the poor, and my family and home duties... As soon as I can, I want to devote myself to some fine and useful work.[67]

Sometimes the busyness of life can be overwhelming, and Elisabeth felt this, too, especially as she also had to contend with her ill health. But she also saw that all this was something she could offer to God, because this was her vocation, her calling, in life:

My God, accept my dispersed life, so often contrary to my wishes – this sometimes fatiguing variety of occupations, acquaintances that do not attract me, cares. Help me to perform all the duties of my state and yet to safeguard my spiritual life. Let the warmth of my welcome, the serenity of my bearing, the friendliness of my words always hide from everyone the miseries of my poor body, and the efforts and sacrifices of my soul. Teach me to be all things to all men, and to be more austere within, to myself alone.[68]

Inner Poverty

Both Elisabeth and Félix came from wealthy families and were wealthy in their own right. Elisabeth realised that a life of poverty was not her vocation, but she could seek poverty in other ways:

Our divine Lord loved poverty: it was His companion from the manger to the Cross. He was Himself poor and lived among the poor, and ever since, many souls, chosen by Him, have followed His example and made poverty the foundation of their life, having adopted it permanently. This is not my vocation, but still I must not forget the very special graces given me by God, nor the consecration of my soul and my life to Him. He has, to some extent, set me apart, and my most earnest desire is that He will deign to make use of me for His own glory and the good of souls.[69]

Elisabeth therefore sought spiritual poverty, 'detachment from all that is purely human', and poverty of heart, not clinging to money, the esteem of others and the comforts of life:

As far as is compatible with my duties in life, I will practice a little poverty. In matters affecting myself alone, I will avoid luxury and self-gratification in dress and occupations. Occasionally I will undertake lowly or somewhat humiliating tasks which I am not strictly bound to perform. I will aim at simplicity in my food, and choose in church and elsewhere a place among the poor, sometimes deliberately setting aside whatever might flatter my vanity. I will efface myself in favour of others, and lead them to forget the advantages of birth or fortune that Providence has bestowed upon me. Even when engaged in good works, I will not put myself forward, but strive everywhere and with all men to be in some small degree one of Christ's poor.[70]

Positive Living

Elisabeth was a naturally positive person, but God's grace sanctified her natural gifts into supernatural gifts. One of her patrons was St Teresa of Avila, who prayed that she be delivered from sad saints. In our secular milieu where there is so much negativity, we need her example:

There is a way of living and thinking that I would call

negative, another that I would call active. The first consists in seeing always what is defective in men and institutions, not so much to remedy them as to triumph over them; in always looking behind one, and in seeking by preference whatever separates and disunites. The second consists in looking joyfully at life and its duties; in seeking the good in everyone in order to develop and cultivate it; in never despairing of the future, the fruit of our will; in feeling for human faults and miseries the valiant compassion that leads to action and that no longer allows us to live a useless life.[71]

The Role of women

Elisabeth thought deeply about the role of women in society, which was soon to change radically. In her times few women went out to work, especially those of her social standing. She strongly supported the Government's new laws on the education of women, but Elisabeth was concerned especially with their moral and spiritual influence in the world. Women were the intellectual equal of men and should use their gifts to enrich society. Her thoughts on duty strongly mirror her own character!:

Woman, whose immense role and influence the French do not yet fully grasp, and who does not always grasp it herself, should from now on realise her task and consecrate her life to it.

To recoil from duty and sacrifice is cowardly. Today, there is a duty to bear children (and it is often a sacrifice); it is a duty to have a care for those in less fortunate circumstances than our own in the matter of wealth or education; it is a duty to develop unceasingly one's intelligence, to strengthen one's character, to become a creature of thought and will; it is a duty to view life with joy and to face it with energy. Finally, it is a duty to be able to understand one's time and not despair of the future.

All this a woman can do. As much as man, she is a being who thinks, acts, and loves; she can proudly reclaim for her right to duty. But for that she must come and draw her strength from the source of all strength, and to increase her intelligence she must bring it into contact with the supreme Intelligence. But this is also true of man. He also is powerless without God.[72]

TO BE AN APOSTLE

Elisabeth started to write a diary in September 1899, and in the second entry she writes of her desire to love those who differed most from her and her desire to share 'what God has placed within me', which was the wellspring of her work among the poor:

> I want to love with a special love those whose birth or religion or ideas separate them from me; it is those especially whom I must try to understand and who need me to give them a little of what God has placed within me.[73]

To be Christian is to be an apostle, and an indispensable part of Elisabeth's spiritual life was her work among the poorest in the fauberges of Paris, her prayer for them and her influence on souls. Elisabeth belonged to two organisations which provided a wide range of support for them. She tried to interest Félix in her work, with little success. He was more interested in overseas missions rather than the need nearest home. Félix saw the delight his wife took in the work as she took him round and showed him everything. He saw the love she had for the children and the genuine affection and love they had for her, the influence she had over them by her calm and gentle firmness, but was not at that point able to appreciate what he saw. She approached those for whom she worked with a deep respect and delicacy which was very much a characteristic of her:

> To go more and more to souls, approaching them with respect and delicacy, touching them with love. To try always to understand everything and everyone. Not to argue; to work instead through contact and example; to dissipate prejudice to reveal God and make Him felt

without speaking of Him … Deep, unalterable respect for souls; never to do them violence, however gentle one tries to be, but to open wide one's soul to show the light in it and the truth that lives there, and to let that creative truth enlighten and transform, without any merit of our own but simply by the fact of its presence in us.[74]

Before Elisabeth began this work, she first reflected deeply on the specific needs of the people to whom she ministered, and how to do this from a specifically Christian point of view:

Reflected a good deal on social questions, which even the most humble of us might help to solve. Social questions are essentially the questions of Christianity, since they are concerned with the place of each man in the world and his material, intellectual and moral improvement. These questions, which will last as long as the world, can advance only through Christianity, that is my absolute conviction. Christianity alone addresses itself to the individual, to that which is most intimate in him; it alone penetrates to the depths of being and is able to renew it.

It is the duty of every Christian to interest himself in the crisis through which people are passing, one which perhaps will change them profoundly. For new needs there should also arise new apostles. The people – the masses that form the majority of the country, these workmen, peasants, and humble labourers of every kind – need to be shown the True Source of every liberty, justice and real transformation. If we do not make God known to them we should have failed in the most important and pressing duty of all. But this is a work that demands forgetfulness of self, a disinterestedness, a persevering will for which we need God and for which we must transform ourselves absolutely.[75]

In this passage she emphasises that social reform, for her, is not concerned with only material well-being, but embraces the whole person in their relationship with God. Also, that it cannot be imposed from outside, without the apostle experiencing his own spiritual transformation first. With her delicacy of approach Elisabeth worked and prayed with a profound desire to work with the grace of God which is unique in every individual soul, as she found in the Gospels:

> Let us go back to the holy source, to the Gospel, the word of God. Let us draw from it lessons of moral strength, heroic patience, tenderness for all creatures and for souls. Let us Christians be sure never to 'break the bruised reed' nor to 'quench the smoking flax'. That reed is perhaps the mournful suffering soul of a brother and the humble flax extinguished by our icy breath may be some noble spirit that we could have restored and uplifted. Let us beware: nothing is so delicate and so sacred as the human soul, nothing is so quickly bruised. Let each one of our words and deeds contain a principle of life that, penetrating other spirits, will communicate light and strength and will reveal God to them.[76]

She recognised that everyone has a vocation, is called by God, and has an indispensable role in the plan of salvation, that only he or she can fulfil:

> The word *vocation* means 'calling': it is God's secret call to the conscience to walk in the path that He has traced. According to the design of Providence, each of us is intended to do some special work assigned to him that is determined beforehand. Human society would be beautiful if each man in his appointed place accomplished all the work set before him by the Master of the household, and if we, labourers of the first hour, tried to discover His will at every stage of our lives.[77]

To work among the poorest is to work without any thought of reward, but to see in them the face of Jesus Christ:

> To know how to understand them will be part of the task, to love them deeply will be another, but to love them for themselves alone and for God, without any expectation of return or consolation, simply because they are persons and because Christ, in looking upon them one day, uttered this loving remark, 'I have compassion for the crowd' (Mark 8:2). Let us also know how to have pity.[78]

Above all, love should be the wellspring of every action:

> Above all we must ask God to fill us with an intense charity. Charity is love: the love of God that renews and transforms the soul and life and becomes the secret cause of our acts, the love of all creatures, the powerful and living love of souls, the love of all that suffers and laments.[79]

Apostolate to the Spiritually Poor

Her concern for souls was not confined only to the materially poor, but she felt that her apostolate was to everyone with whom she came in contact, to the often shallow souls she met with in her own social class. God could turn even the rejection and mockery she met with to his own designs:

> This is perhaps what God especially intends for me. He has treated me like a 'privileged child'; the word has been spoken to me and I know its profound truth; He has arranged everything in me and about me to prepare me for this form of apostolate. In making known to me His intimate and personal action in the depths of the human soul, in obliging me to live in the midst of total negation and indifference and that impenetrable ignorance of divine things that oppresses so many unfortunate people, He has doubtless intended that I

should understand the most widely differing states of mind, that I should have compassion for those who blaspheme and doubt with more pity and love.[80]

I must nevertheless know how to make myself all things to all men and interest myself in things that sometimes seem childish, and which sadden me by their contrast with my own state of mind. Often people are like great children, but Jesus has said that what is done for children is done for Him. So let us show indulgence to childishness and to the incredible light-mindedness of so many about us, and insofar as it is useful, let us learn how to become little with all types of 'little ones', even the little of soul. Let us try to speak the language they can understand, and with them stammer eternal truths. Has not God done the same with us, and has He not placed in our souls only as much light as we can bear?[81]

The little ones, the poor ones, the suffering, can be found in all walks of life. Elisabeth recognised them in the poor with whom she worked and the in the upper echelons of society:

To go always to the little ones, the suffering, those for whom life is hard; but to have no scorn for those light-hearted ones who live for themselves. They more than the others, perhaps, need to be loved, need a little charity to show God to them. Resolutely to devote my intelligence, my will, my heart, all my soul and my being to God, to the advancement of God's Kingdom in the world and in souls. To raise, strengthen, and spread a little of the warmth that He has put into my heart, the 'fire' that kindles me, which I grieve to be unable to kindle in other souls.[82]

With Love, Not Hatred

The Leseurs loved to travel, and this widened Elisabeth's

horizons and her understanding of people different from herself. It pained her profoundly when anyone was persecuted, as she wrote about the Jews during the Dreyfus affair, when a Jewish officer was unjustly convicted of treason. This led to many attacks on Jews, even in Catholic circles:

> Talked to [a close family friend, Emile Alcan] and his wife yesterday about the unjust and unchristian treatment of Jews in certain circles. My God, will you not give to poor human beings a spirit of intelligence and wisdom, which is the gift of your eternal Spirit? Will you not awaken soon in them the spirit of charity that you came to bring into the world, and which you said contained 'the law and the prophets?'. I wish I could organise a holy crusade against hate and promote justice among men and women. At any rate, in this garden God has given me to cultivate, I want to plead by my attitude, my words, and my actions before everyone I meet the great cause of charity.[83]

> Fanaticism fills me with horror, and I cannot understand how it can exist with sincere conviction. Can anyone who loves Christianity passionately and wishes to see it reign in souls think for one moment that he should use any method to achieve this goal other than persuasion? Can one instil conviction through force or deceit? Besides, is there not in the use of such means something completely repugnant to the upright loyal spirit that should mark every sincere Christian? And yet how many little acts of fanaticism we commit unconsciously?[84]

It is so easy to respond to hatred with hate, but for Elisabeth it was an opportunity to respond with love, drawing on the best of Christianity, which should lie at the heart of every Christian life:

> Is it not terrifying to see what the human heart can

easily harbour and reveal of fanaticism and hatred! What thoughts and manly resolutions this unhappy state of things should inspire! A sublime task awaits every upright soul imbued with the ides that Christianity has given to the world – to promote union among men, to sow a little love around one and to give one's time and trouble and all one's heart in order to bring to birth te light and life of the spirit.[85]

Catholic Action, Political Action

Elisabeth studied the books of those who were involved in Catholic action, and wrote to her sister Amélie:

At least there are Catholics who are not hopeless and who do not believe in the restorative power of politics, but who preach the action of words and example. These are hard words, entirely appropriate for the sort of people known as conservative, a good word that deserves to be better applied. He says with reason that when one preaches the gospel to these people and demonstrates to them that society (their society) is anti-Christian, one seems to be revolutionary, and the 'good old times' for which they long are simply the time of privileges and not that, even more distant time, when all classes were imbued with Christianity.[86]

Elisabeth moved among circles in close contact with politicians and was not overly impressed, as she wrote to Charles Duvent:

You see, politics distorts everything it touches, and the electoral advertising forces us into awkward compromises! Certainly, I long passionately that more of peace and happiness would reign among men, but for that to happen we must start at the beginning. How can people who for the most part, hate each other, dream of establishing a universal brotherhood, without first making it live among themselves and in their own hearts? To constitute firmly and in union the family, this basis of humanity, then the homeland, and then, and only then, to seek to establish, more and more, peace and common effort among the peoples; this, it seems to me, is the truth. But to pursue a vague dream of universal love while squandering one's efforts on the common ground, and half opening the frontiers of the invasions of tomorrow, is folly! Let us seek between ourselves areas of agreement, working completely together for the common good.[87]

Duvent, being an artist, could not hep being affected by the ugliness he saw around him, and Elisabeth, too, with her great sensitivity, found it could also drag her spirits down, too:

You speak of my optimism, and what you call such is made up for me of many rough patches, great and small, of sacrifices and sadnesses; I well believe this name does not suit the condition you mean by it. Only – and I say this very humbly, because it is no merit of mine, but a grace – I have a very great and very precious resource. When human beings seem to me to be too wicked, that life and the effort that it calls for a little painful and duty arid; when I sense most keenly that there is in me something of the highest and the best, when I cannot find food for satisfaction in the midst of things and people who despise the good and ignore the beauty; then, I go to the source of all beauty and all truth; I take refuge there, in ardent prayer, close to him who gives the most profound peace; I console myself with the God of humanity and I return a little better and soothed about poor humans, my brothers.

That is why, my dear friend, sorrowful as I so often am, like you, in this contact with the realities of life I cannot become bitter and scornful.[88]

Yes, there is much evil, much meanness in the world, and the great error of the socialists and other reformers is to imagine that through violence, through the theories they develop, humanity will discover how to regenerate itself and enter into an era of endless happiness. These fine illusions last a long time, then comes the time of disillusionment and of discouragement, when one becomes pessimistic and gives up. This is all because the point of departure is false. Besides, as others as well as you have said, even the sincere exploit the situation. Even among the sincere there is often such arrogance, such a desire to play a role, to be the leader, and there is a subtle form of pride among the refined.[89]

Jesus said that the poor would always be with us, but that does not mean that we shouldn't do all we can to tackle evil and suffering:

My dear friend, I am starting from a different point of view. I am persuaded that evil and suffering will never completely desert our poor earth, but I am also convinced that it is everyone's task to work to reduce evil and suffering as much as possible, in our own sphere, humbly, simply, without concern for our precious personality, through dedication, love, the gift of ourselves to that which is our duty. I believe that to accomplish this mission, the first thing to do is to try to become our best selves, even perhaps without knowing it. And God will do the rest. Our effort, our sacrifices, our actions, even the most hidden, will not be lost. This is my absolute conviction; everything has long-lasting and profound repercussions. This thought leaves little room for discouragement, but it does not permit laziness. We are poor day-labourers of life; we sow and God gives the harvest. You understand ... I am unable to despair of humanity.[90]

PRAYER

*Prayer was the vital well-spring of Elisabeth's life, and she
so devised her busy life that there would always be a time for
quiet prayer and reflection, usually first thing in the morning.
She had made in her bedroom a small oratory where she could
pray, defining prayer as:*

> When we pray we remain in a union with God that is
> strong, quiet, and lasting; we look at everything from
> God's point of view, and are so peacefully anchored on
> eternity that annoyances, unavoidable struggles, and
> continual activity have no power to disturb our souls or
> to drag them down.[91]

Prayer is as vital for the soul as is food for the body.

> The life of reason and the supernatural life have not
> the same methods and are not sustained by the same
> food. The soul lives by prayer, just as the intellect
> absorbs intellectual nourishment and the body material
> substances; the soul perishes when it lacks divine
> warmth, just as the body dies for want of food and the
> mind for want of education. Someone has well said that
> prayer is the breath of the soul in God. Let us never
> lose this breath by giving up that inward prayer which
> brings down grace upon us and makes us live.[92]

*At the same time, it is firmly rooted in the material world,
while giving an added dimension to it:*

> When life is established on a solid foundation of
> faith, and we are aided daily by grace, we can dwell on
> earth and do our part in building up society. And, at the
> same time, we can enjoy the happiness and affection

that come in our way, to a degree almost unknown to those who do not bring a little of eternity to bear upon their love and pleasure. Nothing human is foreign to us, and we possess the priceless privilege of being at the same time members of the human race and sons of earth, and also members of the heavenly race and sons of God.[93]

She describes what took place in her prayer, but she also notes that prayer has to bear fruit in action. Although later recognising, when active work was no longer an option for her, that prayer itself is a high and fruitful form of action:

No one knows what passes in the profound depths of our soul. To feel God near, to meditate, to pray, to gather all our deepest thoughts so as to reflect on them more deeply: that is to live the inner life, and this inner life is the supreme joy of life.[94]

Learning to Pray

This prayer can be very lofty, and for many they need to be introduced gently into the practice of prayer. One such was Elisabeth's own mother, a very devout Catholic who shrank at the thought of deeper prayer than she was accustomed to. Elisabeth gives her advice as to how to be introduced into the regular practice of meditation:

I know well enough that your nature shrinks from the thought of contemplation, and that you are alarmed by the very word *meditation*, just as the idea of entering a church would frighten an unbeliever. Nevertheless, you would no doubt tell any unhappy infidel that in the church, where he sees nothing attractive, there is One whom he does not know and that prayer there is more delightful and fruitful than elsewhere. I can tell you the same thing about meditation; the name repels you, but the thing itself is very beautiful and profound, being the foundation of the Christian life.

But meditation has to be approached, and that requires an effort in the first place, to set aside each day the time necessary for it, and further, to force oneself to make a meditation regularly, and to persevere when there is no feeling of pleasure and when God withholds all consolation. It behoves us to take the first steps in quest of God, but if we persevere in seeking Him thus, He will someday give us a hundredfold in return, and the reward granted to our labour is very sweet.[95]

Prayer Needs Structure

It is often not easy to find time for prayer in a busy life, but it is essential if we want to remain in union with Jesus and the things of God. Jesus said 'when you pray', not 'if you pray', taking it for granted that prayer is natural to human life:

Whoever wishes to lead a truly Christian life must first exert his will, and so regulate his existence as to put the most important things foremost. I think that nothing is more important in the use of our days than the time given first of all to God. It may be very short, as a few minutes are enough every morning for us to offer up our thoughts, deeds and word, and all that wealth of sufferings which becomes daily a source of grace to the souls on whose behalf we offer it. ... Add to this ten minutes or a quarter of an hour devoted to reading and meditating on some passage, and your morning and night prayers, and all together they do not amount to one hour given to God out of the twenty-four. Is it really too much to ask of so good a Christian as yourself?[96]

Elisabeth also gave advice to Emile Alcan. Prayer, meditation, needs structure. Jesus said, 'when you pray'...he takes it for granted that prayer is within the very structure of

*being human, and needs application within the framework of
our day, every day:*

Meditation is the withdrawal of oneself into the
very depths of one's being, to that point where, as
theologians tell us, amid the silence of outward things,
we find God; where you will find the source of all
good, strength and beauty (and this is God), where you
will steep yourself in the thoughts of what is eternal
in preparation for the strife of this world, and where
you will understand, as your ideal becomes daily more
clearly defined, both your own weakness and all that
you can do here below in the cause of righteousness.
A very definite subject must be taken for meditation,
which otherwise is apt to become vague and dreamy,
and, in that case, the remedy would be worse than the
evil. Meditation should end in a practical resolution
that can be applied at once; and it should be made
every day, all the more when one is disinclined for it. It
is in time of sickness that one most needs a physician.[97]

A Universal Dimension

*Contrary to atheistic belief that prayer is self-centred and
narrow, Elisabeth realises that it opens up to a Christian
worlds unknown to the non-believer, and therefore makes a
person more whole, because it includes the entirety of what
makes a person fully human:*

A Christian is, therefore, in one sense complete,
for his thought and action may be as wide as that of
the greatest scholar – depending on his intellectual
faculties – and at the same time, the sphere of the
infinite and eternal lies open to him, revealing not only
the world of sense, the knowledge of the changes and
events that take place, but also the infinitely greater and

unchanging world of God and the human soul.[98]

Elisabeth's prayer embraced the whole of her life and had a universal dimension. Although she does not often mention Our Lady, the Mother of Christ had an important role in her spiritual life. She echoes the marriage service, because every soul is a spouse of Jesus, united to him, as were the people of Israel in the Old Testament:

> Receive the renewed gift I offer Thee of myself, my soul, my life, wishing to love and serve Thee alone, joyfully, everywhere, always, with my whole being, wishing to do nothing but Thy Will 'in health or illness, poverty or riches, happiness or suffering, life or death,' asking Thee only to use me as the most humble instrument for the good of souls and for Thy glory.

> May my grief and supernatural joy, my whole life and even my death proclaim the greatness of divine love, the holiness of the Church, the tenderness and sweetness of the Heart of Jesus, the existence and beauty of the supernatural life, the reality of our Christian hopes.

> I believe, I adore, I put myself under the special protection of the Blessed Virgin, and I have the sweet confidence that, offered by her, my humble oblation, with divine grace, will serve the Church, souls, and those who are so entirely dear to me on earth.[99]

Elisabeth makes the important point that we have to develop our intellectual faculties – knowing Jesus Christ, our understanding of the Catholic Faith, advice on prayer and development of the spiritual life. She built up an extensive library of Catholic literature, from the Early Fathers of the Church up to the present, because that gives a sure foundation to belief, as well as giving the Christian the 'armour' to withstand the attacks on the faith. She also loved to immerse herself in the Liturgy and the changing seasons in the Church's life:

Catholic liturgy has great charm for me; I love to live, in the course of the year, the great collective life of the Church, uniting myself with its joys and sorrows, joining my feeble prayers with its prayers, my weak voice with its powerful voice. It is sweet to me to go through the liturgical cycle, reliving our Saviour's life, from His Incarnation to His death and Ascension; through the mouths of the prophets, fathers, and saints of all ages to tell Him my faith and my love; to adore Him in company with those who have adored Him through the centuries; to offer myself to Him with shepherds, disciples, and martyrs, with souls of all times; to feel myself a living cell in the great Catholic union; and to come, after so many others, and before so many who will follow me, with my homage to the Infant God, the suffering Christ, the risen Lord.[100]

Union With Christ

A turning point in her spiritual journey took place during her visit to Rome in 1903, and took her to a new level of union with Christ:

I felt in myself the living presence of the blessed Christ, of God Himself, bringing me an ineffable love; this incomparable Soul spoke to mine, and all the infinite tenderness of the Saviour passed for an instant into me. Never will this divine trace be effaced. The triumphant Christ, the eternal Word, He who as man has suffered and loved, the one living God, took possession of my soul for all eternity in that unforgettable moment. I felt myself renewed to my very depths by Him, ready for a new life, for duty, for the work intended by His Providence. I gave myself without reserve, and I gave Him the future.[101]

The Eucharist

At that time, it wasn't usual for Catholics to receive Holy Communion at every Mass. Elisabeth went perhaps three times a week, and the sacraments of Confession and Holy Communion were vital to her spiritual life and development:

> On Wednesday I had a striking example of what God's grace can do, and I saw how abundantly it is given in the sacraments. I had spent the morning in a state of extreme prostration and sadness; during the day I went to confession, and I was at peace again; I seemed to be – and indeed I was – renewed by a strength other than my own. The sense of forgiveness and spiritual renewal in the sacrament of penance is wonderful. And yesterday morning I received communion with the same peace and the same abandonment to God. I felt Jesus truly living in me, and now I want to become different, to be totally Christian, with all that that word means of self-forgetfulness, strength, serenity and love.[102]

> The Holy Eucharist is indeed food for the soul; to say so is a commonplace, but how true! Apart from the conscious joy it sometimes brings, even lacking that joy, the soul is left stronger and more alive; the Eucharist transforms it, although the soul may not be aware of this mysterious operation at the time.

> This incorporation into us of the divine substance, this assimilation of the Being *par excellence* with our being, this eternal Life penetrating our lives, this close contact with the most holy and tender Soul of all, with this spiritualized humanity, as St Paul says, works within us, and if our will belongs to God, deeply renews us.[103]

She saw in the Eucharist her whole spiritual life: it brought her to the Sacred Heart, to the heart of God burning for love of us. It brought her to Mary, with her maternal protection. It mapped out her life, a hidden life of prayer, sacrifice and service:

> I want to be a Eucharistic soul, a hidden apostle of the divine Heart.to practice complete, confident, and loving abandonment. To go to God by means of the Cross. Through the Heart of Jesus, under the sweet maternal protection of Mary. Whatever it may be, let the future be welcome, since it comes from the heavenly Father and the one Friend. As the future becomes the present, it will bring me its own necessary graces. Until then, and even afterward I must remember that 'sufficient unto the day is the evil thereof' and that the present day is the one during which I can work and suffer for souls, for the glory of God.[104]

The Communion of Saints

Central to her prayer life was Elisabeth's belief in the doctrine of the Communion of Saints. She writes about her belief on the Feast of All Saints, the Feast of the Communion of Saints:

> This is a sweet feast, the feast of those who already live in God, those whom we have loved and who have attained to happiness and light; it is the feast of eternity. And what a fine idea to make the feast of the dead follow so soon! During these two days a vast stream of prayer and love flows through the three worlds: between the Church in Heaven, the Church on earth, and the Church in which souls wait and expiate. The Communion of Saints seems doubly close and doubly fruitful. We feel that all souls and all those we love are close to us in God; and this living dogma by divine grace gives life to many souls on earth and in Purgatory. Not one of our tears, not one of our prayers is lost, and they have a power that many people never suspect.[105]

> *She places it in the context of her central belief in God and the power of intercessory prayer:*

Spoke and discussed a great deal with some dear friends who do not believe. More than others I love these beings whom divine light does not illumine, or rather whom it illuminates in a manner unknown to us with our restricted minds. There is a veil between such souls and God, a veil through which only a few rays of love and beauty may pass. Only God, with a divine gesture, may throw aside this veil, then the true life shall begin for these souls.

And I, who am of so little worth, yet believe in the power of prayers that I never cease to say for these dear souls. I believe in them because God exists, and because He is the Father. I believe in them because I believe in this divine and mysterious law that we call the Communion of Saints. I know that no cry, no desire, no appeal proceeding from the depths of our soul is lost, but all go to God and through Him to those who moved us to pray. I know that only God performs the intimate transformation of the human soul and that we can but point out to Him those we love, saying, 'Lord, make them live.'[106]

> *She writes to Emilie Alcan, an unbeliever, to show how this belief also has its counterpart in the natural order:*

Every Christian believes that there is a mysterious, supernatural connection between himself and all the other children of the same Father. By virtue of this connection, which we call the Communion of Saints, the efforts, the merits and sufferings of each individual benefit all the rest. A similar Law exists in the natural order, and if we reflect a little, we shall be convinced that our words and deeds have a much more profound and far-reaching effect than we are apt to suppose. Hence it is an absolute duty for everyone who understands what *absolute* and *duty* mean to refrain from doing or saying not merely what is bad, but also what is indifferent, since there can be no neutrality in matters of morality.[107]

We know that nothing is lost, either in the material or spiritual world, and that the lowliest of our actions, the most secret of our prayers, has immeasurable force, for it echoes on through time and space, and it may be that, ages hence, some human hearts may be brought into mysterious contact with us.[108]

On the visit to Rome in April 1903, Elisabeth had an experience of what the Communion of Saints meant in practise. Writing to Charles Duval, who was in Rome painting a portrait of the new Pope, Pius X, she spoke of meeting the previous Pope, Leo Xlll, who had died three months after her visit. Although she was in the midst of her fellow Catholics, she recognised that the Church, the Body of Christ, embraced far more than her professing members:

I recall that almost transparent old man, clothed in white, with lively but profound eyes, with a noble gesture, his long transparent hand raised in blessing; the acclamation of the crowd, and I experience once more the overwhelming sense I had at that moment. An inner happiness, an inexpressible sweetness, and I felt myself a member of that great living body which is the Church, of being united as one in that vast community, and a participation in that life which circulates in Christianity and, because of him, united in one same love, not only for those, like me, who are a part of the body of the Church, but of all those souls of good will.[109]

The Expansive Force of Love

Nothing that we are or do is insignificant, because in the mystery of salvation every act of ours, what we are, affects others. Therefore, we should strive for the best, the best that, with the grace of God, we can be, so that we will become part of that 'great expansive force' of love:

> I believe that in good there is a great expansive force; I believe that no humble, unknown act or thought, seen by God alone, is lost, and that all, in fact, serve souls. I believe, according to a saying I love, that 'when we do good we know not how much good we do.' What we have to do is to work on ourselves, to accomplish our own inner transformation, to do each day and each hour our duty and all the good that we can do.[110]

Elisabeth had love and concern for everyone with whom she came in contact. Through prayer, she was united with those she would never meet on earth. Because each one was precious to God, then they were precious to her:

> Let us seek them, understand them, and love them, from the soul of the maidservant in our house, and those that are shrouded sometimes under a ridiculous or gloomy exterior; to those distant and unknown souls that can nevertheless be affected by our prayers and sufferings, although it is only in eternity that they will learn how our passing sorrows or our humble sacrifices have won for them life everlasting.[111]

The Transformed Life

Prayer cannot help but spill over into daily life – and it must - and have an effect on one who prays. Elisabeth is a prime example of this, and her unbelieving friends also recognised that something special in Elisabeth herself. While describing it as she saw it in the close friends who worked with her among the poor; she strove for it herself and it admirably describes what she herself had become:

They are rare, no doubt, but there flows from them such an intensity of inner life, such calm strength, such true beauty that merely to come into contact with them soothes and comforts us. After all, this is only natural. Our outer life is the reproduction of our inner life, and the visible part of us reflects what is unseen; we radiate our souls, so to speak, and, when they are centres of light and warmth, other souls need only to be brought into contact with them in order to be warmed and enlightened. We give out, often unknown to ourselves, what we carry within us; let us strive to increase daily this reserve store of faith and quiet charity.[112]

If prayer spills over into ordinary life, it is also deeply embedded in it. It is a common misconception that people of faith have to dress differently, behave differently – while not engaging in activities that could lead into sin, but for Elisabeth there was no contradiction:

People in the world do not realise that one can be very detached from all human things and live a keen spiritual life, and yet find sweetness in the interests, occupations, and joys of life. However, it is only when one has rooted oneself in eternity that one can let one's humble little barque float upon the surface of the waves and rejoice fully in the view from earthly rivers. Storms no longer frighten one; the clear sky makes one more bold. The sun is always shining behind the clouds; the light, the beauty, does not conceal the eternal and splendid light that guides us to port and waits for us there.[113]

SUFFERING

Elisabeth had great physical suffering all her life, from when she had hepatitis as a child, which left her with internal ulcers, to when she contracted the breast cancer from which she eventually died. As she was gradually unable to continue her apostolic work she recognised that she had a new apostolate, that of prayer united with her suffering:

> More and more I see that God does not want me to be active, unless a new state if affairs should arise. What He seems to expect from me is an apostolate of prayer and suffering. What a blessed vocation, and how much I will try to respond better to it than in the past, loving the Cross of Jesus, 'carrying it daily', always placing in the divine Heart my burden of pains, privations and weaknesses! Austere to myself, I want to have nothing but sweetness and tenderness for my neighbour. To live in interior spiritual union with our Lord, and to make of all the monotony, triviality, and humble duties of my life so many prayers for souls. To have a Eucharistic soul, never to lose sight of my vocation of prayer, suffering and reparation.[114]

> Oh, so long as it is the divine response to me – is it not so, Lord? And so long as no least part of my pain is lost! Stronger than my poor action, stronger than my imperfect prayer, may it reach Your Heart and become the most efficacious form of supplication.[115]

She experienced all the problems of dealing with long-term illness, finding in Holy Communion the grace and strength she needed:

A long time of illness, during which I could only live united by the deepest intimacy of my soul with God, forcing myself to accept and offer Him my sufferings. May He let them serve in expiation of my faults and accept all my intentions for them.

Most painful privation of many spiritual helps not able to go to Mass. And yet, great joy, for the Saviour comes each week, to visit me [in Holy Communion] and brings me, with the sweetness of His presence, a strength I could never have alone. There are so many painful things in the empty monotony and distraction of those times when we are ill. God alone can make of this emptiness, of these little sacrifices and successive privations, a work of redemption for me and for others. Is there no sweetness in being on our Saviour's Cross and, so close to Him, obtaining the grace of salvation or conversion for others, for souls that are greatly loved?[116]

The Pain of Rejection

She offered her pain and suffering for the conversion of souls. But another suffering was to see her love meet only with rejection. Perhaps this was one of the things that caused Jesus to agonise in the Garden of Gethsemane:

There is little suffering that can compare with this: to love, and to be repaid with hatred or at least hostility; to dream of doing good for someone, of giving part of oneself, and to find that this person does not appreciate you, judges you unfairly, and misunderstands everything about you. What should one do then? Not to be unjust in return; remember that the Master suffered misunderstanding and contempt; and, without reproaches or sorrowful thoughts of self, continue to speak, to act, and love, not to gain the affection denied us, but in the higher and supernatural thought of charity.[117]

The Pain of Loneliness

Perhaps her greatest suffering was that she was unable to share what was most precious to her with Félix, and the loneliness of soul and spirit this entailed. She loved solitude, but not isolation:

> I love interior solitude with God alone; it strengthens my soul, and gives it light and fervour again. But sometimes isolation, which is a different thing entirely from solitude, weighs it down.
>
> I thirst for sympathy, to bare my soul to the souls that are dear to me, to speak of God and immortality and the interior life and charity.[118]

She suffered greatly from inner loneliness, unable to share with him whom she loved best, her husband, the faith that burned within her; unable to share it, except in rare instances, with those in her circle of family and friends:

> Unite with my soul the souls of those I love, the soul I love best of all, and put an end to this grievous solitude of spirit, which weighs on me so much. And then, sanctify me, too, by this suffering, bring me close to Your Heart and teach me to love and serve You better. I resolve (imploring divine grace) in the future to give way no more to the lapses I have known in hours of extreme pain, to be always gentle, humble, full of charity.
>
> Help me, dear Saviour.[119]

Thankfully, the Lord answered her prayers for what Elisabeth called a 'soul sister', when the family stopped off at the Hôtel Dieu, a famous hospital that catered for the terminally ill, on the way to Jougne. There she was to meet Sr Goby who, like her, was seeking a soul sister, and the two found the friend they were looking for.

The Pain of Bereavement

Elisabeth also suffered greatly the pain of bereavement, in a time when many children died young. Her youngest sister, Marie, died of typhus at the age of twelve, and her sister, Juliette died 13 April 1905; this death, of one whom Elisabeth called the friend of her heart, affected her even more deeply. It was only after three months that she could put her grief into words, marking the date of her death only with a black cross:

It is three months exactly since I wrote these last lines and uttered the cry of anguish that Thou hast heard, O my God. Thou hast not granted the supreme prayer that went out from my tortured heart, or rather, Thou hast granted it differently and better. All that I desired for my beloved (with what ardour Thou knowest!) all that I had hoped for her of human joys and health and sweetness, all the life that I had begged Thee to allow her, and the final happiness, all these Thou hast given to her in taking her, in drawing her, to Thyself.

Oh, I cannot believe that my constant ardent prayers, and those of others for her, and all the sacrifices offered and the tears shed, and so much suffering accepted, could all be useless. I do not believe that all her trials, her life of privation and grief ended by a sweet and holy death, could be without fruit.

If earthly happiness was denied to her, if she knew bitter trials and separations, and if in the end she was taken from us, it is that a better life awaited her than on this earth, it is that joy out of all comparison with her cruel suffering was prepared for her by the God of love, and that God wished her to know all beauty and all good and to give her His light, and that her dear soul was purified and holy enough to enter into the domain of sanctity.[120]

Let us learn to smile at all that he sends: joy or sorrow, illness, consolations or heavy dryness of spirit, even these meannesses and – this is for me – these little social obligations and all external things that weigh heavily on a soul that longs more and more to be with God. There is in the depths of me an ardent desire for withdrawal, of a hidden, silent life that the world and even some Christians do not understand.[121]

God is Always There

In times of spiritual darkness, of bodily suffering, of external difficulties, it is easy to think that we have slipped back in our journey to God. But, as Elisabeth experienced, looking back, she could see that God was guiding her by unseen ways:

When a poor wayfarer is climbing up a steep and difficult path, he sees only what is immediately before him, and the means of overcoming or avoiding each obstacle as it occurs; he forgets the road already traversed, and thinks of nothing but the stones which bruise him and the brambles which tear his hands. But when he is higher up and able to halt, he turns around and looks back upon the way that he has come, and perceives that, in spite of his doubts, blunders, and weariness, he has advanced by unknown paths toward a goal determined beforehand and that the sun, with its lifegiving heat, is rising above the horizon.[122]

My Saviour, I am all alone, as Thou knowest, in spiritual things; Thou knowest, too, what I suffer from the hostility or indifference of certain persons. I think that is why Thou hast done so much for me and given me so much in Thy goodness. And now with Thy gentle gaze Thou hast dispersed the clouds that in these last months have often darkened my soul; Thou art kindling it again after leaving it in painful aridity; Thou art chasing away the shadows and the confusion. I give

Thee thanks, my beloved Saviour, my God! I know that grief will return, for effort and struggle are Thy will for the souls Thy love hast conquered; but I know that Thou wilt not abandon me and that deep peace will remain with me. To love amidst the storm is very sweet, and my love emerges stronger from each sorrow, each setback. Complete abandonment of myself to Thy will; offering of my heart and my life in Thy service and for souls.[123]

Towards the end of her life, Elisabeth could look back and see how God her Father had guided her all through her life, and despite her interior and exterior sufferings, there was a peace and a light so deep within her that nothing could disturb:

By God's grace I have reached this point; the road has been traversed, and, as I look back, I see again the various stages through which my soul has passed, and I recognise, in the guidance of my life, a will that is steadfast, unchanging, and harmonious, and a love so fatherly that I am able to believe in Divine Providence after seeing it, so to speak, at work in my life and heart. The great, true sun has risen above the horizon of my soul, and all the clouds of suffering fail to obscure its brightness, while it has tinged them with its divine radiance. My wish is to live and die in its light, veiled now so that our poor mortal eyes may endure it; but I look forward to the full glory of that light in eternity, when I shall be reunited with those whom we have loved so dearly and shall love forever.[124]

ELISABETH AS OTHERS SAW HER

To her atheist friend Félix Dantec she stood at the peak of humanity, and when Yvonne, his wife and Elisabeth's friend became anxious or worried, he would tell her to go and take a bath in Elisabeth's serenity. Serenity was a virtue that Elisabeth tried to cultivate all her life and was so obvious to all with whom she came in contact. Her friend Aimée Fiévet described her impressions of Elisabeth during the discussions that took place among their friends, often in a hostile atmosphere:

> When she did not approve of a judgment, an idea expressed and she had reason to keep silent …. She neither protested by an expression on her face, nor by critique. From her silence emanated something inexpressible giving the impression that she had withdrawn into her soul, like putting something away in a safe place.
>
> She was a good listener, looking for the truth or wisdom of her interlocutor. Some discussions were very profound and prolonged … At other times in intimate conversations, her face took on an extraordinary appearance, as if she wanted to understand completely what was being said …. and expressed it, especially if it was a matter of education, morality, or duty, etc. If they did not come to agreement, she would end …. easily, with a smile full of resolve and hope and say, 'we will think about this each from our own side'. Elisabeth was very clear-sighted and intuitive, often understanding something that had not been said. If she thought she might be helpful or useful, she would make the perfect response with discretion, without giving the impression of an intrusive intimacy.[125]

Elisabeth longed for a 'soul sister', one who could fully appreciate her desire for holiness, the value of suffering, her desire to put her Christian faith into action. She found this in Sister Goby, When they finally met the sister recorded her first impression of Elisabeth, and the prayerfulness that radiated from her:

I had seen the radiance of that same spirit on your face when I saw you near the tabernacle of our little chapel when I approached you for the first time!

I found it again shining through the features of your face and expressing itself in our conversation in our intimate hour in the morning! And then, oh! instantly I loved you and felt so attracted to you! Yes, I want my soul to become a true Sister to yours.[126]

Félix described her as the perfect hostess:

Physically she was very attractive, with ways and manners full of distinction, and a kindness that made her always welcoming, smiling and amiable, a perfect hostess – in short, the accomplished mistress of her house. Being greatly drawn to young people, who repaid her affection fully, she had made her home a centre of warmth and gentility. As eagerly frequented as she was herself sought out.[127]

Félix himself appreciated the effect she had on others, and how people were drawn to her:

With a mind open to everything, remarkably quick and penetrating, she rejoiced in everything beautiful in nature or in the genius of man … Her conversation was lively, interesting attractive, and spirited, but always simple and modest, without ever making a show of her intellectual superiority. She was thoroughly gay and took care to be so always; she even considered gaiety a virtue … Her lovely laughter rang out at every opportunity, with its fresh, frank sound.[128]

Félix noticed the effect she had on other people, a gift for friendship and the affection in which she was held:

She was also a rare friend, in whom might be found a singular power of affection. This was very apparent in the last years of her life. Her state of health then necessitated great care. We went out hardly at all and entertained very little; she paid no more visits, and frequently spent the days stretched out in her invalid's chair; and yet visitors flocked to her, and never perhaps was her company more sought out. I sometimes even dreaded the fatigue that might result from these long talks. She had become more and more the centre of attraction, and there is nothing more touching and even consoling to me than to think of the anxious sympathy that surrounded her during the last months of her life, and the vivid and tender remembrance – a veritable cult, - in which she is held by all those who knew her.[129]

Elisabeth's death 3 May 1914 was not the end of her story. It is to be hoped that her example of a holy life lived in the world with all its preoccupations, challenges and opportunities, may eventually see her raised to the altars, an example of a lay person living in the world and dealing, especially, with the hostility to the Christian faith which is becoming ever more prevalent.

Endnotes

[1] Elisabeth Leseur, *My Spirit Rejoices,* (Manchester, New Hampshire, Sophia Institute Press, 1996), pp. 117ff.

[2] Elisabeth Leseur, *Journal d'enfance,* (Paris, Editions du Cerf, 2012), pp.81ff.

[3] *Ibid.,* p. 94.

[4] *Ibid.,* pp. 99ff.

[5] *Ibid.,* p. 100.

[6] R.P. M-A (Felix) Leseur, *Vie d'Elisabeth Leseur,* (Paris, J. de Grigord, Editeur, 1946), p. 85.

[7] *Ibid.,* p. 86.

[8] *Ibid.,* p. 95.

[9] *Ibid.,* p. 108.

[10] R.P.M. Leseur *Vie,* p. 110.

[11] *Ibid.,* p. 119

[12] *Ibid.,* p 122.

[13] *Ibid.,* p. 123.

[14] Elisabeth Leseur, *My Spirit Rejoices,* p .50.

[15] *Ibid.,* p.51.

[16] *Ibid.,* p. 45

[17] *Ibid.,* p. 148

[18] *Ibid.,* p. 211

[19] J. K. Ruffing RSM (edited, translated and introduced by), *Elisabeth Leseur* (New York: Classics of Western Spirituality, Paulist Press, 2005), p. 191ff.

[20] Elisabeth Leseur, *My Spirit Rejoices,* p. 205.

[21] *Ibid.,* p. 119.

[22] *Ibid.,* p. 120.

[23] *Ibid.,* p.116

[24] *Ibid.,* p. 104.

[25] *Ibid.*

[26] *Ibid.,* p. 79

[27] *Ibid.*

[28] *Ibid.,* p. 158.

[29] J. K. Ruffing RSM, *Elisabeth Leseur,* pp. 165ff.
[30] *Ibid.* p. 166
[31] E. Leseur, *My Spirit Rejoices*, p. 89.
[32] *Ibid.,* p. 107.
[33] *Ibid., p. 100.*
[34] *Ibid.,* p. 145.
[35] *Ibid.,* pp. 73ff.
[36] *Ibid.* pp. 93ff.
[37] *Ibid.,* p. 62.
[38] J. K. Ruffing RSM, *Lettres sur la Souffrance,* (Paris, Les Éditions du Cerf, 2012) p.41.
[39] *Ibid,* p. 57.
[40] R. P. M.-A. Leseur *Vie,* pp. 198ff.
[41] J. K. Ruffing RSM, *Lettres sur la Souffrance* p.153.
[42] *Ibid.,* p.176.
[43] *Ibid.,* p.162.
[44] E. Leseur, *My Spirit Rejoices*, p.153.
[45] R. P. M.-A. Leseur *Vie,* p. 351.
[46] *Ibid.,* p. 19.
[47] *Ibid.,* p. 23.
[48] E. Leseur, *My Spirit Rejoices,* (Manchester: New Hampshire, Sophia Institute Press, 1996), p. 237.
[49] *Ibid.,* p. 148.
[50] *Ibid.,* p. 51.
[51] *Ibid.,* p. 119.
[52] J. Ruffing RSM), *Elisabeth Leseur,* (New York: Classics of Western Spirituality, Paulist Press, 2005, p. 220.
[53] *Ibid.,* p. 211.
[54] *Ibid.,* pp. 47ff.
[55] E. Leseur, *Light in the Darkness,* (Manchester New Hampshire: Sophia Institute Press, 1998), p. 112.
[56] E. Leseur, *My Spirit Rejoices* p. 120.
[57] J. Ruffing RSM), *Elisabeth Leseur* pp. 211ff.
[58] R. P. M.-A. Leseur (Félix Leseur), *Vie d'Elisabeth Leseur,* (Paris: J. de Gigord, Editeur, 1946), p. 232.

[59] E. Leseur, *My Spirit Rejoices,* p. 114.

[60] *Ibid.,* p. 110.

[61] *Ibid.,* p. 104.

[62] *Ibid.,* p 116.

[63] *Ibid.,* p. 113.

[64] *Ibid.,* p. 170.

[65] *Ibid.,* pp. 240.

[66] E. Leseur, *Light in the Darkness,* p. 45.

[67] E. Leseur, *My Spirit Rejoices,* pp. 62ff.

[68] *Ibid.,* p. 152.

[69] E. Leseur, *Light in the Darkness,* p. 69.

[70] *Ibid.,* p. 76.

[71] *My Spirit Rejoices,* p. 208.

[72] *Ibid.,* pp. 52ff.

[73] *Ibid.,* p.45.

[74] *Ibid.,* p. 79.

[75] *Ibid.,* pp. 55ff.

[76] *Ibid.,* p. 47.

[77] E. Leseur, *Light in the Darkness,* p.118.

[78] *My Spirit Rejoices,* pp. 70ff.

[79] *Ibid.,* p. 48.

[80] *Ibid.,* pp. 118ff.

[81] *Ibid.,* p. 86.

[82] *Ibid.,* p. 61.

[83] *Ibid.,* p. 63.

[84] *Ibid.,* p. 205.

[85] *Ibid.,* p. 208.

[86] R. P. M.-A. Leseur, *Vie d'Elisabeth Leseur,* pp. 252ff.

[87] *Ibid.,* p. 158.

[88] Ruffing RSM, *Elisabeth Leseur,* pp. 165ff.

[89] *Ibid.,* p. 166.

[90] E. Leseur, *Light in the Darkness,* p. 109.

[91] *Ibid.*

[92] *Ibid.,* p. 116.

[93] *Ibid.,* p. 109.

94 *Ibid.*, p. 36.

95 *Ibid.*, p. 37.

96 *Ibid.*, p. 46.

97 *Ibid.*, p. 133.

98 *Ibid.*

99 E. Leseur, *My Spirit Rejoices*, p. 169

100 *Ibid.*, p. 145.

101 *Ibid.*, pp. 73ff.

102 J. K. Ruffing RSM (edited, translated and introduced by), *Elisabeth Leseur* (New York: Classics of Western Spirituality, Paulist Press, 2005), p. 78.

103 E. Leseur, *My Spirit Rejoices*, p. 121.

104 *Ibid.*, p. 185.

105 *Ibid.*, p.101.

106 *Ibid.*, pp. 54ff.

107 E. Leseur, *Light in the Darkness*, p. 43.

108 *Ibid.*

109 R. P. M.-A. Leseur (Félix Leseur), *Vie d'Elisabeth Leseur*, p. 23.

110 E. Leseur, *My Spirit Rejoices*, p. 48.

111 *Ibid.*, p. 92.

112 *Ibid., p. 100.*

113 *Ibid.*, pp.152, 153.

114 E. Leseur, *My Spirit Rejoices*, pp. 186ff.

115 *Ibid.*, p. 193.

116 *Ibid.*, pp. 133ff.

117 *Ibid., p. 231.*

118 *Ibid., p. 62.*

119 *Ibid.*, p. 104.

120 *Ibid.*, pp. 93ff.

121 E. Leseur, *Lettres Sur La Souffrance,* (Paris, Editions du Cerf, 2012), p. 111.

122 E. Leseur, *Light in the Darkness*, p. 84

123 E. Leseur, *My Spirit Rejoices,* pp 170ff.

124 *Ibid.*

[125] J. K. Ruffing RSM *Elisabeth Leseur*, p. 192.
[126] *Ibid.*, p. 170.
[127] E. Leseur, *My Spirit Rejoices,* p. 8.
[128] *Ibid.*
[129] *Ibid.*, p. 9.

BIBLIOGRAPHY

B. Chovelon, *Salt and Light*, (San Francisco, Ignatius Press, 2020)

E. Leseur, *Journal d'enfant*, (Paris, Les Éditions du Cerf, 2012)

E. Leseur, *Lettres a des Incroyants,* (Paris, Les Éditions du Cerf, 1928)

E Leseur, *Lettres Sur La Souffrance*, (Paris, Editions du Cerf, 2012)

E Leseur, *Light in the Darkness*, (Manchester, New Hampshire, Sophia Institute Press, 1998) Leseur, *My Spirit Rejoices*, (Manchester, New Hampshire, Sophia Institute Press, 1996)

J. Ruffing RSM, *Elisabeth Leseur* (New York: Classics of Western Spirituality, Paulist Press, 2005)

R.P.M-A Leseur, *Vie d'Elisabeth Leseur*, (Paris, J. de Gigord, 1946)

J. Moorcroft, *When Silence Speaks,* (Leominster, Gracewing, 2019)